GROUP DISCUSSION

More than 100 topics covered

- Simple yet effective techniques to prepare you for any Group Discussion
- Solutions to some common problems of the students
- Do's and Don'ts of a GD
- Tips on facing the troubles that may arise during a discussion
- Frequently asked topics, abstract topics and some latest topics
- Mock GDs

Nitin Sharma

UNICORN BOOKS

Publishers
UNICORN BOOKS
F-2/16, Ansari Road, Daryaganj, New Delhi-110002
☎ Ph.: 011-23262683, 23250704, 45644782
E-mail: info@unicornbooks.in • *Website:* www.unicornbooks.in

ISBN 978-81-986503-7-5
Group Discussion (More than 100 topics covered)

Author: Nitin Sharma

Edition: 2025

Printed at : Param Offsetters, Okhla, New Delhi-110020

A Word from the Author

Hello friends,

Welcome to the exciting world of Group Discussions! A group discussion is your gateway to a lucrative career, as many esteemed organisations use it as a tool to select the candidates with the desired traits (and reject the ones with negative traits). B-schools, BPOs and various companies in various fields conduct group discussions. Perhaps, that's precisely the reason why you are holding this book right now. But if you are one of those persons who don't like group discussions very much, let me assure you that you are a part of the majority. In fact, it will be very hard to find a person who never felt a tingling sensation in the body or butterflies in the stomach before or during a group discussion. Yet, I must say that a group discussion is nothing to fear of! It won't be an exaggeration to state that group discussions are a part of our day-to-day life. Perhaps you have never had a day when you didn't discuss anything with anyone. Every time you talk to someone, probably you are amidst a discussion. You may be discussing the inaugural F-1 race of India, the latest movie of your favourite superstar, your career plans, or a relative's health, or any subject at hand; and these discussions prepare you for the professional group discussions. Then why do we feel nervous before a professional GD? Because the stakes are high. A good performance can make your career, while a not-so-good one can break your long-cherished dream. And how can you overcome this nervousness? The answer is simple: By preparing for what may come. The very purpose of this book is to prepare you for any group discussions you may have to face. All the techniques described in this book are simple yet effective. As you go through the book, you will feel more and more empowered. And never forget – Practice makes a student perfect. All the best!

– NITIN SHARMA

Contents

1. Group Discussion – Understand It to Master It 11
2. Types of Group Discussions 14
3. Preparation Matters A Lot! 16
4. Special Tips for Those Who Hate Group Discussions 19
5. How to Perform Well in A Group Discussion 21
6. How to Shoot Troubles in A Group Discussion 27
7. What If You Still Fail to Perform in A Group Discussion 30
8. Mock GD – Complete Performance Analysis of Ten Candidates 31
9. Three More Mock Discussions 36
10. Some Important Topics 55
    1. *Globalisation* 55
    2. *Global Warming* 57
    3. *AIDS* 59
    4. *Science – Boon or Bane?* 61

5. *Euthanasia (Mercy Killing)* 63

6. *Capital Punishment (Death Penalty)* 64

7. *Reservation in Jobs/Education* 66

8. *Co-education* 68

9. *Love Marriages and Arranged Marriages* 69

10. *Nuclear Power: A Gift or a Curse?* 70

11. *Social Networking Sites are Harmful to the Society* 72

12. *Brain Drain* 73

13. *Vegetarianism* 76

14. *Multi-tasking* 78

15. *Effects of Video/Computer Games on Children* 80

16. *Great Leaders are Born, Not Trained* 82

17. *Work Hard or Work Smart?* 83

18. *Are Strikes Justifiable?* 84

19. *Time is Money* 86

20. *Red* 87

21. *Blue* 89

22. *Green* 90

23. *Black* 91

24. *White* 92

25. *Black and White* 93

26. *Red vs. Blue* 95

27. *Gold* 96

28. *Old is Gold* 97

29. *Is the Ban on Plastic Bags in Cities Justified?* 99

30. *Internet: A Boon or A Bane?* 100

31. *Control Over Social Networking Websites – Justified?* 101

32. *Freedom of Press – Why is It Important?* 102

33. *Rapidly Growing Population of India – A Boon or Bane?* 104

34. *India-Pakistan Relations* 105

35. *India-China Relations* 107

36. *India vs. China* 108

37. *BRIC/BRICS* 110

38. *OPEC* 110

39. *SAARC* 111

40. *Unity in Diversity – A Gift or A Curse?* 112

41. *Reservation for Women in Politics* 114

42. *Deforestation* 115

43. *Domestic Violence* 117

44. *Dowry System in India – Should We Get Rid of It?* 120

45. *The Commonwealth* 121

46. *Delhi Commonwealth Games, 2010* 122

47. *Cricket – A Game or A Religion?* 123

48. *India's Olympic Dreams* 124

49. *Public Transport in the Indian Cities* 127

50. *Preserving Our Historical Monuments* 128

51. *Security of Women in the Indian Cities* 129

52. *Ethics in Business – Why Are They Important?* 131

53. *Family or Career?* 132

54. *Time Management* 133

55. *What is More Important – Process or Result?* 134

56. *Pollution in Our Rivers – What to Do About It? (or 'How to Save the Ganges, Our Sacred River?')* 135

57. *Air Pollution in India* 137

58. *Terrorism in India* 138

59. *Corruption in India* 139

60. *Artificial Intelligence – Can It Replace Human Intelligence?* 141

61. *Indo-US Nuclear Deal* 142

62. *Should India Sign CTBT?* 143

63. *Right To Information Act (RTI Act)* 145

64. *Agni-V* 146

65. *We Need Food for Everyone, Not Missile (or 'Missile or Infrastructure?')* 147

66. *High Oil Prices – What Can People Do About It?* 148

67. *Doctors' Work – Service or Business? (or Hospitals as Business Centres?)* 149

68. *Child Labour – Is It Wrong?* 150

69. *Effects of Cinema on Youth* 151

70. *Capitalism, Communism and Socialism* 155

71. *Linking of the Rivers in India* 157

72. *Pokhran Nuclear Tests – Have They Helped Us or Harmed Us?* 158

73. *Honour Killing* 159

74. *Is Sex Education Important?* 161

75. *Cloning – Is It Ethical?* 162

76. *Should Large States be Divided into Smaller Ones?* 164

77. *Money is Needed to Make Money (or Money Begets Money)* 166

78. *Linking Religion and Politics – Is It Okay?* 167

79. *Food Adulteration in India* 169

80. *Vision-2020 for India* 170

81. *Mass Migration Towards the Metros in India* 171

82. *Criminalisation of Politics* 173

83. *Group Discussion* 175

84. *Education – A Business?* 177

85. *God Particle 'Higgs-Boson' – Does It Explain God?* 179

86. *India's Economic Growth* 180

87. *Inflation in India* 181

88. *Should All the Public Sector Undertakings (PSUs) be Privatised?* 184

89. *Disaster Management in India* 186

90. *Tourism in India* 188

91. *Manager and Entrepreneur* 190

92. *'Whole is Greater Than the Sum of Its Parts'* 191

93. *Online Shopping Websites – Their Future in India* 192

94. *Illiteracy in India* 195

95. *Poverty in India* 196

96. *Is Education System of India Effective?* 199

97. *IT Sector of India* 201

98. *BPO Jobs as Career* 203

1

Group Discussion
Understand It to Master It

"Nothing in life is to be feared. It is only to be understood." – Marie Curie

What is a Group Discussion? Why is it conducted?

Many students believe a group discussion to be a loyal friend; many others think it's a formidable foe. Let me assure you, it is neither. In fact, it is rather a simple process in which participants sit together and discuss a topic, and try to reach a consensus (or solution to a given problem). Group discussion is conducted because before an organization recruits a candidate, it wants to make sure that the candidate is suitable for that particular job. For instance, if it's a sales job, the candidate must have a right mix of assertiveness and willingness to serve the customer, so that he or she can sell the product and retain the customers. If it's an administration related position, the candidate must be able to display confidence. A B-School conducts a group discussion to select the candidates with managerial traits. These traits can be easily spotted during a professional group discussion, as there is time pressure in addition to the pressure to perform. Nevertheless, a candidate, who has practised enough, can perform under any amount of pressure.

Why should you love it?

To a large extent, your success depends on your attitude. It is a universal fact that the more you love something, the better you get at it (and vice-versa). Therefore, if you want to perform well in a group discussion, learn to like it (yes, it can be learned!). Those who hate group discussions are less likely to perform well in them. (Moreover, why should you hate something neutral? Why not love it instead?) Change this tendency as soon as possible. How? I'll tell you. The more you understand something, the more you love it. Therefore, keep practising until you learn to love it. Trust me, it will pay off well in the end.

Group Discussion Myths

Myth 1: You should always initiate the discussion: Though it is true that you may earn some points if you take initiative, but you should only do it if you know the subject well. A weak opening (because of poor knowledge of the subject) may work against you and may give a wrong impression of your leadership qualities. I won't say that first impression is the last impression, but first impression does matter a good deal. So, if you are not confident enough, let someone else take the initiative and then you can make your points. However, I'll advise you to be among the first few speakers.

Myth 2: Only aggressive speakers win: Nothing can be further from the truth. Aggression is one thing, assertiveness is another. And you can be assertive without being aggressive. While aggression may diminish your chances of getting selected, assertiveness may enhance your chances. Just back your statements with relevant examples and arguments.

Myth 3: You should speak very loudly so that others can hear you: You should speak loud enough, but not too loudly. Shouting is not considered appropriate. In fact, the most successful speakers hardly ever shout. Speak as naturally as you always do when you talk to the people. ('How to make yourself heard in a fish-market' will be discussed later.)

Myth 4: If you speak a lot, your chances of getting selected are increased: It's simply not true. Saying irrational things will leave a bad impression on the evaluator (judge). Even if you have a lot to say, say it in a concise manner. Let others also make their points. It shows team spirit. (However, that doesn't mean you should cut back on your time so that others can speak. Live and let live.)

Myth 5: If you speak like a celebrity, you'll make a great impression: Please don't underestimate the evaluators. They want to hear you, not a famous personality. Be yourself.

Myth 6: If you keep quiet, you may still get selected: No chance. No pain, no gain. You have to say what you must, or how else will the judges evaluate you?

Myth 7: Only fluent speakers perform well in a GD: Fluency has its benefits, no doubt. But even if you are not an absolutely fluent speaker, still you will have a fair chance if you know what to say and how to say it. Your knowledge, attitude, manners, attentiveness and other qualities also determine your score. (That doesn't mean you can ignore the fluency part entirely. Work on it as much as you can, but don't take unnecessary tension. In fact, some B-schools arrange language fluency lessons for those bright candidates who need them.)

Myth 8: You may use your native language in a GD: Some people believe they can do this. No, you mustn't. While an evaluator may forgive some of your mistakes, speaking in your native language will definitely leave a negative impression, unless, of course, it is also the official language of the discussion. However, you may use a few words or examples which are very common and generally known to all. Otherwise, stick to the language allowed to you (which is mostly English).

Myth 9: The group must reach a consensus: No. Though it is good if the group does reach a consensus, but it is not a condition (unless stated so by the organizers). Evaluators know you may not have sufficient time to reach a consensus. Just do your best.

❑❑❑

2

Types of Group Discussions

'An investment in knowledge pays the best interest.' – *Benjamin Franklin*

1. **Topic-based discussion:** You can be provided a topic which is:

   (a) A controversy: For example, your topic could be *'Caste-based reservation'*, or *'China – Biggest threat to India?'* or *'Which diet is better – vegetarian or non-vegetarian'*, etc. In this type of discussion, you are required to take a stand on the given topic, and support your stand with suitable arguments and examples.

   (b) A descriptive one: For example, you may be told to discuss 'Indo-US Relations', or 'Poverty in India', or 'Causes of Inflation'. In this kind of discussion, your knowledge of the subject plays an important part. Else, you may be provided a plain fact and told to discuss it.

   (c) An abstract topic: This type of discussions has gotten popular in the recent years. Topic may be anything under the sky, such as 'Zero', 'Black', 'Gold', or a number, or anything you can think of. Your creativity comes into play here. You simply say what you think is relevant about the topic.

2. **A case study:** You may be given a real-life situation or an imaginary case scenario, or even a dilemma. Then you'll be asked

to present your opinion on the given situation, or find a solution to a given problem (as a group or/and as an individual).

You may be instructed to speak one by one or all at once, or even both. Such variations hardly matter to a candidate who is well prepared.

❐❐❐

3

Preparation Matters A Lot!

'Before anything else, preparation is the key to success.'

– *Alexander Graham Bell*

How to prepare for Group Discussions: Some simple and powerful techniques

- **How to practise with friends:** If you were thinking that you need to cut back on the time you spend with your friends to prepare for a GD, think again. In fact, group discussions are one of those few tests in which your friends can help you a lot. Every time you're discussing something with them, you're preparing for a GD. However, you need to set apart some time to discuss the topics which are commonly asked in GDs. We have provided a list of such topics. Ask your friends to discuss them one by one, taking at least one or two every time you meet. This exercise will be even more helpful if you have a mentor watching you, so that you don't divert from the topic. They may also provide you invaluable feedback. Use an alarm clock (or the alarm in your mobile phone) to keep track of time. After the discussion, ask your friends to give an unbiased feedback of your performance. Try to minimise the mistakes pointed out by them next time you're discussing. Also, at least once a week, try to look as formal as you will be in a real discussion. Dress formally, act formally and think formally. It will make you feel more comfortable on the D-Day. One last point: Don't include those friends in such discussions, who don't take the discussions seriously. You may meet them other times. What? None of your friends wants a serious discussion? Let's see what else you can do in that case. How about your classmates?

- **How to practise in a class:** A class seems to be the perfect place for formal discussions. And why not? You have almost everything you need for a group discussion available in a class. You can rearrange the chairs (at least after college hours), use blackboard, and avail the help of your professors (at least those who are friendly with the students). Moreover, you can definitely find the students with similar goals. Spend some time with such students after college hours. Just take care that you notify the group when to meet and in which room to meet. Practise as described in the revious paragraph. Again, take care to include only the serious participants who want to learn something.

- **How to practise with family members:** If one of your family members has gone through the process of group discussions, you're lucky. Ask them to discuss something with you (that 'something' could be anything – a breaking news on TV, a newspaper headline, or even anything related to their profession). Even if they have been out of practice for years, at least they can listen to you when you speak and provide their feedback. They'll be more interested if you choose a topic related to their field of work.

- **Using TV and Internet to your advantage:** There are so many news channels on TV and hundreds of useful websites on the internet that can help you enhance your knowledge about the current and historical topics, and can also teach you how to express your thoughts clearly. Watch discussions and debates on the news channels. Some popular ones are 'The News Hour' on Times Now, 'Hard Talk' on BBC World, 'Centre Stage' on Headlines Today (there are always some nice debates/discussions on the news channels these days). If you love internet, search

'Group Discussion' on any search engine and you'll find almost all the information you want. On 'YouTube', you can find recorded discussions. If you're looking for information, search Wikipedia. There are more ways available today than ever before were.

- **Make your mobile your true friend:** In most of the mobile phones, you get the 'recording' option (or else you can use a tape-recorder). That means you can record your own voice and play it back to know how you sound when you speak. You can use a stop-watch to check your pace. Although some experts say that a particular pace is most suitable to make others understand your point, but trust me, a real GD can be very unpredictable! May be you'll get a plenty of time to make your point, or may be others will keep interrupting you. That's why, in my opinion, you should be able to change your pace according to the situation. If you get sufficient time, speak at your natural pace. If it's a hell out there, you may have to speak a bit faster. Prepare for both. The following exercise will definitely help you: Take a book, find a nice paragraph (preferably a part of your favourite leader's speech), read it at your natural pace and then at a faster pace, record both, judge whether you were able to make it understandable both times. Do it as many times as you want. It will help a lot.

- **How to practise alone:** Stand in front of a mirror and try making a short speech (it need not be longer than 1-2 minutes). Watch your expressions as you speak. Watch your body language. May be you should use your hands more/less, or may be you should keep your chin a bit high! Watch the way you dress; your colour combination, knot of the tie, shoes, etc. Notice every big and small detail. Make changes as you desire. Remember, the more you sweat in practice, the less you bleed in a fight (or a GD).

Three words for you – practice, practice and practice. The more prepared you are, the less tense you'll be on the D-Day.

❑❑❑

4

Special Tips for Those Who Hate Group Discussions

'The best way to destroy an enemy is to make him a friend.' – Abraham Lincoln

There can be many reasons for why you hate group discussions. May be you are an introvert person; may be you think you can't get through it; may be you have a BP issue! And it is also true that the number of people who hate group discussions is quite high. But since you can't afford to hate it, here are some tips for you:

1. Begin your preparations as early as possible. You should try to get better at discussions. When you do something well, you begin to like it. It's a well-established fact.

2. When you practise in front of a mirror, try to speak like your favourite speaker/news anchor/politician sometimes. Think why they love to speak. If you like this exercise, if it helps you, continue it. *(Caution: This exercise is only for practice, till you fall in love with GD. In a real GD, be yourself.)*

3. Make your GD practice a fun. For instance, when you're working on fluency, speak the dialogues you like. It will make the activity more appealing to you.

4. Go in depth of expected topics; try to find more and more about them. The more you know an issue, the more you can speak on it.

5. Learn to admire yourself. No matter how bad you perform, you'll still be more courageous than those who simply watch and laugh at others. As you might have heard, you never fail if you try. Every performance prepares you for the next one.

6. Don't worry about the stage fright. Almost everyone has it. It tends to fade away with time.

7. If you have the problem of high BP, take your medicine regularly and act natural in a GD. There's never a need to get overexcited. Trust me, there have been the performers who don't shout at all and still perform extremely well. Only after enough preparations you'll be able to do this.

8. In GDs, there's always a second time. Don't care so much about your performance that it gets on your nerves.

❑❑❑

5

How to Perform Well in A Group Discussion

It is quite common for the students to feel a bit nervous on a crucial day; be it an exam, a GD or a personal interview. It's okay to feel butterflies in your stomach. However, you can ward off unnecessary nervousness if you keep track of certain things. Here's what you should do before and amidst a real GD:

What to do before a GD?

1. Take adequate sleep the night before GD.
2. Do not try to read too much before a GD. Preserve your energy for the main event.
3. If possible, read the headlines in the newspaper. Go through the major ones. May be they can provide you some good points for the day's discussion! It will have a positive impact on the evaluators if you're able to cite an example from the day's news.
4. Needless to say, dress well. You should look as professional as possible (some people confuse professional with artificial; please don't!).
5. Reach the venue one hour before the set time. Make sure you're carrying all the required documents. Also take along a water bottle. Add glucose to it if you want. If you find other candidates already waiting there, it might be useful to talk to

some of them (at least to those who like to talk). It may help you overcome any nervousness you might be feeling. You can even make some good friends!

6. Sometimes you may be asked to introduce yourself to other candidates. So, keep a brief introduction ready in your mind.

7. Do as you are directed. When your turn comes, take a deep breath, relax and enter the room. Some people find it useful to warm up by mildly stretching their bodies before a GD.

Remember, other candidates also have their weaknesses just as you do; you'll find them during the GD. Stay confident.

DO's and DON'Ts of a GD

1. Be who you are. Never try to be someone else in a GD.

2. If you are well-acquainted with the subject, initiate the discussion. However, if you are not confident about it, don't initiate. But try to be among the first one-third of the speakers.

3. It is a good strategy to start with a unique question/statement (sometimes called 'startler'), but make sure it is relevant to the subject given.

4. Be assertive. Make your point strongly. It shows leadership qualities. However, don't be rude or interruptive. Listen to others too. It shows you can work in a group.

5. Appreciate the good points made by others. It shows your team spirit, and can also fetch you some support in the discussion.

6. Don't shout even if somebody else is shouting. Maintain your calm and composure all the time.

7. Some people say you should hide your emotions during a GD. I partly agree. However, at some point, you'll feel compelled to say something. All you need to do is express your emotions in a sensible manner. Just don't get carried away by them. But it's

okay to smile a bit at some point or express your dissatisfaction over a view at some other point. As long as it is within limits, it can be a part of professionalism.

8. Don't get nervous even if someone is speaking better than you. Do your best and forget the rest. Usually, more than one candidates are selected from every group.
9. Maintain your body language all the time. It shows confidence.
10. Encourage others to speak. It's another trait of leaders.
11. If you haven't been able to understand a point made by someone, ask for clarification. It shows you're really interested in the discussion. However, avoid asking unimportant questions.
12. Use easily understandable words. Don't use passive voice too much. Avoid the words and jargons that only you can understand.
13. Provide relevant examples to support your points.
14. If the discussion goes off track, try to get it back on track; and do that politely and strongly.
15. Try to conclude the discussion in the end.
16. When given a controversial topic, take a balanced approach. Appreciate good points made by others, but stay firm on your stand. Choose your stand wisely.

Now, we will discuss the roles you can play in a GD. A good participant will be able to play more than one of the following roles in any GD.

Roles you can play in a GD

1. **Initiator:** If you initiate a discussion and introduce new points in the discussion, it shows your confidence, ability to take initiative, and creativity. An initiator will definitely gain some points over other members, provided he starts the discussion well.

2. **Info-seeker:** When you ask other group members relevant questions on the points they have made, you become an information seeker. Asking questions can fetch you some points, but don't overdo it; or it might give an impression that you don't have sufficient knowledge of the subject.

3. **Coordinator:** When you help keep the discussion on track, when you make sure that all the important points are discussed one by one, when you show the relations between various ideas presented, you become a coordinator. But remember, unless you prove your knowledge in the initial phase of the discussion, other participants may not accept you as a coordinator. Moreover, to an extent, a coordinator is expected to have an influential personality. If you could prove that you are a good coordinator (in addition to being a good team player), you can expect to get wonderful points.

4. **Elaborator:** When you elaborate upon the points and ideas presented during the discussion, when you provide examples to support them, you become an elaborator. It requires having a good knowledge of the subject to play this role. But if you manage to do it, you are rewarded well.

5. **Opinion giver:** When you give your opinion on the points made by other members, you become an opinion giver. However, you must only play this role in addition to other, more important ones (initiator, elaborator, etc.), because being an opinion giver alone doesn't hold much value. So, it's more like a secondary role that can fetch you some additional points. Nevertheless, if your opinion can change the opinion of the group, the rewards can be nice.

6. **Critic:** Being a critic doesn't mean you need to criticize other group members; it simply means that you have to make an unbiased assessment of the points made by them. When done in a polite manner, it can be quite helpful to the group and make a

good impression on the evaluators. But if you're just a critic and play no other part in the group, you will definitely attract a lot of criticism from the rest of the group, and that will be detrimental to your own image. So, play your cards carefully.

7. **Energizer:** When you act as a stimulator and motivate the group to act in a more energetic manner and in the right direction, you are an energizer. When done in a positive and cheerful manner, it can definitely be a positive trait.

8. **Summarizer:** When you summarize a discussion, you become a summarizer. To play this role, you should keep track of the points discussed during the discussion. You need to tell the group what important points came up and what conclusion can the group reach, or if no consensus was reached. Needless to say, you need to be an active participant throughout the discussion to play this important role.

As we discussed earlier, a good candidate will be able to play multiple roles during a discussion. Some of the qualities and traits you need to display during a discussion are – enthusiasm, assertiveness, team spirit, ability to take initiative, firmness (not rigidity), curiosity, logical thinking, up-to-date knowledge, attentiveness, ability to think under pressure, decision-making and good communication skills, etc. Some points are kept reserved for each of these qualities. Similarly, if you display negative qualities (like lack of attentiveness, aggression, indecisiveness, lack of team spirit, etc.), you lose points. And here's the good news – When you are focussed on your positive qualities, the negative ones may not show at all! So, instead of worrying about the negative, focus on the positive.

Caring by not caring 'too' much

We know how much the success in a group discussion matters to you. But think this way – What if your tendency to care too much makes you nervous during a group discussion and degrades your performance? A renowned negotiator, Herb Cohen advises people to care but not THAT much. Similar thing can be said about a GD. No matter how important it is to you, don't let it get on your nerves, and don't get emotionally attached. Remember, no chance is last chance. When you participate with a free mind, you naturally perform well. It's okay to feel a bit nervous, but why take unnecessary tension? Some candidates can't even sleep the night before the GD! Remember, performance, not stress, is your goal. Focus on GD without wasting your precious energy on stress.

❑❑❑

6

How to Shoot Troubles in A Group Discussion

- **When you are given a topic you don't understand:** Many participants fear that they might be given an unknown topic to discuss. Though it happens very rarely, yet it may happen. For instance, not everyone understands the meaning of 'Euthanasia' (mercy-killing). So, what can you do when you encounter a tough situation like this? Simple, wait for someone else to introduce the topic. When one or two speakers have already spoken, you will be well-acquainted with the topic. Then you can present your opinion. Whenever you have a doubt whether you understand the true meaning of the topic, never be the initiator. A wrong beginning can cost you an opportunity.

- **When someone is trying to dominate you:** Some people would want to step over you and climb the ladder. You do meet such people in life and in GDs. Well, it is easy to tackle them. All you need to do is not to lose your composure. Just don't pay attention to them. Take your own course; not the one they want you to take. Evaluators are experienced enough to recognize true talent; you should trust their abilities. Moreover, they will be happy to select a candidate, who can take unfair criticism in a positive manner.

- **When someone in the group is shouting:** Remember, such persons are annoying to everyone in the group, not only to you. No need to advise them. Let the evaluators evaluate them. However, if you want to say something when someone is shouting, it can be a good strategy to appreciate any good point made by them and then adding what you want to say. You may want to go like this – 'I appreciate you made this point, my friend. In fact I'd like to add that... .' Never try to change the other members; that's not your job.

- **When there's a total chaos:** Sometimes, a group discussion can be compared to an Indian fish market; everyone starts shouting at the same time. When nobody is willing to listen to anyone, it might be a good strategy to stay quiet until the shouters lose their energy and quiet down a bit. At that point, you can enter the discussion. Alternatively, you can start speaking in a steady and monotonous voice until the shouters give in and listen to you. At that point, you resume your natural tone *(an example – "ALL-I-WANT-TO-SAY-IS India can tackle the problem of ...")*. These are the two strategies that work in a fish market. If you want to play a coordinator, you can ask the group members to speak one by one instead of all shouting at the same time (but it may not work when no one is listening to anyone).
- **When someone offends you:** There may be the immature elements, who don't mind pointing finger at anyone, without thinking about the consequences. If it happens once, you may choose to ignore it; if it happens again, you may politely say 'Sorry, but I'm not bound to answer your questions' or 'Since we have limited time, I can't respond to you on this point'. Whatever you say, say it politely but firmly. Remember, you are there to impress the evaluator, not an offender. As a well-known thinker, George Bernard Shaw once said, "I learned long ago, never to wrestle with a pig. You get dirty and besides, the pig likes it."
- **When things seem to be going against you:** This point is not about talking in favour of or against the given statement. I'm talking about a painful but possible situation when other

participants, due to some reason, start refuting every point you make. (Remember, everyone will not turn against you for no reason. Try to identify the reason and eliminate it. May be you have said something offensive; may be you have given an impression that you are not confident about the points you made. Try to reverse the damage.) Well, if you know what you have said, back your points with suitable examples. However, if you have been wrong, then admit your mistake as soon as you realise it. Do it in a cheerful manner, without being too apologetic. There's no point further supporting a wrong stand. However, stay firm on the correct points you made. To win back some support from the group, support the right points made by other members. It will help you make a comeback.

- **When, surprisingly, everyone is calm and composed:** It is more like a dream, yet the dream may come true. If you want to stand apart in such a discussion, play an energizer. Stay cheerful (genuinely cheerful) and motivate the quiet members to participate more. Do it calmly yet enthusiastically. Yes, it is possible to be enthusiastic without being too excited.

❑❑❑

7

What If You Still Fail to Perform in A Group Discussion

Sometimes nightmares do come true. Nobody expects things to go bad, but sometimes they do go. A candidate may fall ill a day before the discussion, and may not speak well. Or one may not perform due to some personal problem despite all the practice and efforts (for instance, if one's mind is preoccupied with a relative's illness). A failure may come due to any reason. If that happens, the worst thing you can do is 'give up'.

How did you learn to ride a bicycle? I'm sure you lost balance and fell down many times. You got up and tried again and again. What if you had never got up and tried again after falling down once? Think. As I said before, no chance is the last chance. Some of the greatest business leaders were once denied a chance by the famous educational institutes. Some of the greatest athletes suffered worst injuries, and still became champions. Read any good motivational book and you will find similar stories. Remember, you are not defeated unless you accept defeat. Moreover, there are many good institutions and companies; not just one or two. Worthy people are always in demand. You may try again; as many times as you need! Never surrender to the setbacks.

❑❑❑

8

Mock GD

Complete Performance Analysis of Ten Candidates

(Ten candidates, some excited and others nervous, are awaiting their turn. They aspire to get admission into the prestigious MBA program of a leading institute. They have been shortlisted for Group Discussion on the basis of their CAT scores. They are wearing badges of their names on their coats, just according to the procedure set by the institute. Suddenly, they notice eight candidates coming out of the discussion room. Now, it's their turn. Since they are the last lot, they all form a single group. An employee of the institute calls out their names one by one and they enter the room, and find three evaluators waiting for them. They are asked to take their seats. After that, one of the evaluators writes a word on the board – **'ZERO'**. *"Here's your topic. Please discuss. You have fifteen minutes," he says. Some candidates look clean bowled. Zero? What is there to discuss about it? Suddenly, one of them starts speaking...)*

Abhijeet: Friends, Zero is a unique number. You multiply any number with it and you get a zero. Due to such unique properties, it is the easiest one to multiply or divide with *(looks nervous)*. We can discuss the mathematical properties of Zero in detail.

Vaibhav: Well said my friend, but we shouldn't forget that zero is more than just a number because it reminds different people of different things. For instance, Zero may remind us of our 'Zero tolerance policy' against terrorism. Zero is also one of the most important discoveries of ancient India. Let's discuss all the important ones one by one. I'd like to begin with 'Zero tolerance policy', if you all agree.

Rajan: Why don't we begin with a lighter one; for instance, if a batsman scores a zero in a match, he's called a duck!

Lakshmi: I think we better begin with 'Zero tolerance policy'. We can discuss the lighter ones if time remains. Please go ahead Vaibhav.

Vaibhav: Thank you, Lakshmi. 'Zero tolerance policy' is adopted against certain crimes which are believed to be unacceptable for the society. 'Zero tolerance policy' means that those who commit certain crimes must be awarded the pre-determined punishments; no matter who they are and why they had committed that crime. Since terrorism results in the deaths of the innocent civilians, many of the top leaders of India have declared that India will have a 'zero tolerance policy' against terrorism. This means that perpetrators and supporters of terror will be brought to justice, regardless of who they are and if they have done it for the first time. I fully agree with this stand because terrorism must not be given a free hand at all.

Shrikant: I fully agree with you, my friend. However, since terrorism is not the only unpardonable crime, we should adopt the same policy against other severe crimes such as rape, murder, drug dealing, female foeticide as well. Everyday we hear new incidences of these crimes on the news channels. Such crimes are against humanity, and the people who carry them out must not be forgiven, no matter what excuses they make.

Lakshmi: I tend to agree with both Vaibhav and Shrikant on this matter, but we must exercise caution while using such a strict policy. Not all the criminals are professionals. What I mean is that some of them do deserve a second chance. For instance, a young person, who has been caught carrying drugs, may not understand the consequences of his actions. Law should allow him to live a respectful life and he should not be given severe punishment; he can even be pardoned for the first time. So, technically, I'm suggesting that, in some cases, 'zero tolerance policy' must consider the circumstances of the person.

Sonal: Friends, since we have limited time, I think we should move on to the next interpretation of Zero. Zero signifies nothingness too, and, as they say, nothingness or emptiness is considered everything in some religions; they believe that when you have attained the state of nothingness, there's nothing left to be achieved anymore. Therefore, it might be...

Rajan: Sorry, but that sounds quite foolish. I mean how can you say nothingness is everything?

Sonal: To make it more clear, I'll use an example. Think of meditation. When you attain the state of no thoughts in your mind, you attain the highest degree of meditation. It means that the state of zero thoughts may be everything for a meditator.

Lakshmi: I think that's a unique and wonderful interpretation of zero.

Vaibhav: And as I was saying earlier, zero is one of the most important discoveries of ancient India. Earlier, it was called *'Shoonya'* in Sanskrit language. It made the number system much more useful and easy to use. Without zero, how could we have developed in the field of science?

Sonal: I'd also like to add one more point about zero. It is believed that our universe started with a big-bang which originated from nothingness, that is, zero! So, zero is much more complex than it sounds.

Shrikant: You're absolutely right.

Rajan: Shall we now talk about the point I raised in the beginning? As I was saying, when a batsman scores zero, we call him a duck. Also, when an actor fails to impress the people, he becomes a zero from a hero. Isn't that funny?

(Nobody says anything.)

Lakshmi: I think we should know the opinions of other group members who haven't spoken so far. Naveen, would you like to add something?

Naveen: I think I agree with all my friends. Nothing more to say.

Shweta: Me too. You have already discussed everything.

Vaibhav: Abhijeet, you were discussing some Mathematical properties of zero, weren't you?

Abhijeet: Yes, being an expert of Maths, I want to say something. Zero is a unique number because it's neither positive nor negative. Also, in Physics, zero temperature is the freezing point of water, while in the Binary System used by all the modern computers, 'zero' and 'one' are the only numbers used.

Lakshmi: Wow, that's really very interesting, isn't it?

Raj: Yes, indeed.

Shrikant: Friends, it's about the time. So, we can conclude by saying that zero is a unique number, more complex than it initially looks, and it holds various interpretations in different subjects and in the minds of different people. Thank you!

[What else could have been discussed – Zero tariffs! Why didn't anyone say that we need to have free trade with some nations in order to boost export and import? Mostly, the candidates with business or commerce background will bring up this important point. (Read more about it in the topic 'SAARC'.) May be someone could have discussed 'zero to hero' stories of real people; or how a student feels when he/she gets a zero in a test; or how accidents happen when the speed of a vehicle is brought to zero in a short time interval; or even how a 'size zero' is considered unhealthy by the health experts. *(Never say you have nothing to add to a discussion. There's always something you can add. Just think with a cool mind.)***]**

[Since the topic given was a difficult one, not all the participants could perform well. Still, those who dared, will reap the rewards.

In the given discussion, Abhijeet made a hasty decision and started the discussion without thinking sufficiently. He may not be selected, except if the selectors want the students with good knowledge of science subjects, which is not likely to happen in most institutions. Vaibhav, the second opening speaker, has successfully put his best foot forward and while making his points in a strong manner, he was able to take other participants along with him. He kept contributing to the discussion and also motivated other members to speak. Therefore, he is very much likely to get selected. Rajan looks a bit arrogant and immature and fails to impress anyone (Don't be surprised by what or how he spoke; you may meet such speakers!). Lakshmi has done a nice job. She put forth her opinion in an assertive manner, and showed that she was able to think independently. She also tried to bring in those who didn't speak. She is very likely to get selected. Shrikant spoke less, but he made his point clear and was able to conclude the discussion; therefore, he has fair chances of getting selected. Sonal did contribute to the discussion, though she began late. However, she has done her job and might get selected for the PI. Raj and Naveen have clearly lost their chances by not contributing anything, while Shweta has proved to be unprofessional too. The tenth candidate could not say a word.]

❑❑❑

9

Three More Mock Discussions

[DISCUSSION I]

(Eight candidates have occupied chairs arranged on both the sides of a rectangular table. The evaluator is seated in the chair at the far end of the table. Students have been given the topic **'Female Foeticide and Girl Child Abandonment'**. *They have been given two minutes to prepare their points; then they will have to speak for two minutes each. After everyone has finished, they will discuss the topic among themselves for the next ten minutes. Students need to introduce themselves and tell their degrees and hobbies before they speak on the topic. The preparation time is almost over and the first student begins to speak...)*

(Note: Although few institutes conduct such a rigorous process of group discussions, nevertheless, you must stay prepared.)

Student 1 (Preeti): Good Morning friends, I'm Preeti. I hail from New Delhi. I have done B. Com. My hobbies include reading motivational books and playing badminton. *(She pauses for two seconds and then continues)* I believe that female foeticide and girl child abandonment are two sides of the same coin, because the underlying cause in both is the same – Some people prefer a boy child over a girl child. I strongly believe that it's not only a crime against humanity, but it also goes against the common sense, because we no longer live in the dark ages when the girls could only stay home and take care of children. Now they move out and do almost everything that men do. They earn for their families, they serve in the armed forces, they even enjoy the topmost posts such as that of the Prime Minister and the President of India, and they still take care of their children! Therefore, it's completely baseless to abandon a girl child or to kill her before she steps into the world. In fact, I'm not able to understand how people can bear to leave their own babies on roadside! This has never been the culture of our nation; actually, such awful incidences malign the image of our nation in the world. The people who do such things are definitely a danger to our social norms and values, and they must be dealt with strongly. That's all I would like to say at this moment. I hope you all agree with me. Thank you!

Student 2 (Richa): Good Morning everyone! I'm Richa from Chandigarh. I hold a B. Sc. from the Delhi University, and I love to read good non-fiction and listen to Pop music. *(After a moment's pause)* We have been given a burning topic to discuss. While it is quite evident from many news reports that girl child abandonment and female foeticide are prevalent in our society, the phenomenon is not new at all. It has been happening since decades, or perhaps centuries, that people either sacrifice or abandon a girl child for a boy child; and this has led to a very irregular sex ratio in many states of our country. According to an estimate, we have only nine hundred and forty females against every one thousand males in India, while the data of child sex ratio is even more disturbing. Only Kerala has more number of females than males. It is very disheartening to see that some people do not want a girl child despite the fact that it was women who gave birth to them. As Ms. Preeti rightly said, such incidences are stains of dishonour on the image of our country. Women need not prove themselves again and again, as they have already done that many times. I believe that we already have sufficient laws to stop these crimes, and what we actually need is effective implementation of those laws. In addition, we will have to work very hard to create awareness among people, because many people still don't understand that a girl child is a gift and not a burden. I have nothing more to add at this moment. Thank you!

Student 3 (Abhinav): Good Morning friends! I'm Abhinav and I come from Karnal. I'm a law graduate, and I love to draw cartoons and play Chess in spare time. I totally agree with Ms. Richa that we already have strict laws to end the menace of female foeticide and to prevent people from abandoning girl child; though there is still room for improvement in some sections. The sex ratio in various states is definitely a matter of grave concern. The matter becomes even more serious when we find that even the economically and socially forward states have not been able to mend the ratio gap. The major reason behind this menace is that we have failed to stop the greedy doctors, who carry out unethical practices like female foeticide and illegal sex determination using ultrasound, despite that some state governments have announced rewards for those who bust such practices. If such doctors were put behind the bars, we could definitely have stopped these crimes from happening, because punishment acts as a deterrent against crime. Apart from creating awareness and strengthening our law and order, what we need to do is create an environment conducive to free communication between common man and law enforcement agencies like police and the courts, so that people will not fear reporting these incidences to law, and this will help these agencies to punish the guilty ones in time. As the first speaker, Ms. Preeti had rightly said, these incidences are against our very culture, which even compared women with revered Goddesses once. Thank you.

Student 4 (Vijay): Friends, I'm Vijay from Delhi and I have done B. Com. I love to play and watch cricket and I've played up to the state level. I have listened to the other speakers, and I doubt whether we are making a mountain out of a molehill. It is a personal decision of a couple whether they want to have a son or a daughter. Who are other people to interfere? *(Some participants wanted to respond immediately but they didn't, because it's not their turn yet.)* I think we should let the parents of the children decide whether they want a girl or a boy child, and not interfere in their personal decisions; especially when we don't know their social or economic conditions. As far as child abandonment is concerned, it's altogether a different issue and I oppose this crime. That's it!

Student 5 (Rohan): Good Morning everyone! I'm Rohan. I hold master's degree in Arts, and I love to play chess in the spare time. While I agree with the other speakers, I can't agree with Vijay at any cost. He's been very wrong in saying that it is a fundamental right of the parents to decide whether they want a girl child or a boy child. Who gives them this right? The Indian constitution? No, it doesn't. They may decide for the future of their children, but not about having only boy children. It is against human values to carry out the hideous crime like female foeticide and child abandonment. I don't know what Mr Vijay was thinking about when he made such a foolish statement. Thank God, he doesn't support girl child abandonment! *(Although angry, Vijay wants to respond immediately, but he doesn't. Nevertheless, his body language and facial expression betray him and reveal his anger.)* I strongly support taking concrete action against the families and the doctors who participate in such crimes. It will even be better to punish some of them severely in order to set examples in the society. There's also a need to make strict laws against these people. Thanks a lot! *(He sits down, staring at Vijay, who's still staring at him.)*

Student 6 (Deepak): Good Morning dear friends, my name is Deepak and I have done BBA from Kanpur, the city I belong to. As far as my hobbies are concerned, I like to cook delicious food and play table-tennis. I can see that nearly every one of us has agreed on a point that we all oppose the illegal practices of sex determination and female foeticide and girl child abandonment. We all want our law and order to play a better role in stopping such crimes. The falling ratio of girls in the country is definitely a matter of concern and I hope that not only our government will play a decisive role in normalizing it, but the people, especially the vigilant and powerful people of our society, will also help the law. I would like to mention Amir Khan's show 'Satyamev Jayate' here. I think we should have more of such shows on TV. In one episode, this issue was raised vigorously, and in the following weeks, some governments had taken the steps to ensure the safety of girl children in their respective states. I think that show must prove to be just the tip of the iceberg, because if we really want to fight these social problems, we will all have to come together and participate in the action. It will be a great idea to carry out candle marches in all the cities of our country. Also we should try to make it a national issue. Let's save our nation's prestige. That's all from my side at this moment, thank you very much!

Student 7 (Ankita): Good Morning everyone! My name is Ankita and I come from Mathura. I have done B. Com. from Bangalore, and my hobbies include reading fiction and writing poems. Friends, while working as a women's rights activist, I found that many women do not want to abandon a girl child, but their family members compel them to take such a ghastly step. We should give a voice to such women who commit these sins under others' pressure, and create special agencies which can provide these women full protection when they reveal something. I fully agree with Deepak that we should make it a national issue and create more and more awareness in the society, until people start dreading the thought of committing such gruesome crimes. In fact, we had once organized a rally against girl child abandonment, but, unfortunately, not many people came out to participate in that rally. But if the well-known people start participating in these rallies, I'm absolutely sure that more and more people will come out and support such causes. And not only the cities, but the villages must also conduct marches to protect girl children. I also believe that it is not a mere coincidence that the state which has the highest literacy rate also has the highest number of females per thousand males. Education plays a crucial role in the awareness of the society. It is high time we acted against these crimes. Thank you!

Student 8 (Vinod): Good Morning friends, I'm Vinod from Raigarh and I have done M. Com. I like singing and dancing. I agree that girl child abandonment and... and female foeticide is a serious crime and we should all be against it. Since everything has already been said on the topic, I will not say much and... That's all. Thank you for the opportunity. Thank you! *(sits down nervously.)*

Examiner: Since everyone has spoken once, I open the discussion to everyone. You have ten minutes. Go ahead!

Ankita *(grabs the opportunity immediately)*: Friends, since we all know each other's opinions now, let's discuss the solutions to the problem of female foeticide and girl child abandonment. Do we all agree?

Preeti: Sounds like a good idea. Please go ahead.

Vijay *(intervenes)*: Hold it guys! When I don't even consider it a problem, how can you say let's discuss the solutions? If female foeticide is a problem, then why have the inventors created the facilities like ultrasound to determine the gender of a child in the first place? It is a personal decision, and...

Rohan: Mr Vijay, why is it difficult for you to understand that ultrasound is only meant to be done when there's a genuine need for it, such as severe pain, etc.? Let others discuss the topic even if you don't want to.

Vijay: I'm not talking to you, Rohan!

Deepak: Friends, we barely have ten minutes in hand! Please keep the personal differences aside and add to the discussion. I think Ms Ankita should go ahead with the solutions.

Richa: Right. Ankita, please go ahead.

(Seeing the support that Ankita has got from other participants, Vijay has no option but sit quiet.)

Ankita: Thanks friends! As I mentioned earlier, it is essential to gain support of influential people in order to make the campaigns against female foeticide successful. The aim of creating awareness must be in the centre of our efforts. This is the only way to completely eradicate this problem.

Richa: Pardon me, but I think it's a better idea to focus on tracing the culprits and bring them to justice. Not everyone listens to pleas. Moreover, this way we can not only discourage the people who tend to commit such crimes, but we can also create awareness faster.

Rohan: Oh, how so?

Richa: See, it's a well-known fact that people tend to avoid punishment. If they come to know that people are being punished for a certain crime, they talk about it more; and that way the awareness is created quickly.

Preeti: My friend, I partly agree with you, but I still believe that it is better if people stop these crimes not due to the fear of law but by listening to their own conscience. I think that would be a truly permanent solution to this problem.

Richa: But Preeti, it may take a very long time to change the hearts of people. Till then, we have to depend on laws, don't you agree?

Preeti: To this I agree. Till the time everyone understands the value of the girls in the society, we have to depend on laws.

Deepak: In addition, what we need to do is to change the typical backward belief that if no boy is born, the lineage of clan will terminate. Moreover, some people consider boys as 'bread-earners' or 'strong gender', that's why they prefer them over the girl children. This dark-age mentality must change.

Abhinav: My friends, we should also take into account the dowry factor. People fear that if they have a girl child, they'll have to save a lot of money for dowry; and, on the other hand, if they have a boy, they will get a lot of dowry money. I think this is why people prefer a boy child. Though we have effective laws against dowry as well, once again the implementation part is weak.

Vijay: Hey Mr know-it-all, dowry is not all wrong. If people give gifts to their daughters, what's wrong with that.

Abhinav: Sorry, but I don't agree with you. What is wrong is wrong. We have to follow the law.

Vijay: So you don't have any answer?

Abhinav *(coolly)*: I think we are not bound to answer personal questions here.

Richa: I think more and more states must declare rewards for those who report incidences of female foeticide. In addition, the whistle-blowers must be provided sufficient security. These steps will encourage people to report such crimes.

Abhinav: Good suggestion. In fact, I would like to suggest a similar idea. If our society resolves to boycott the wrong-doers, it can be a better motivation than monetary rewards.

Deepak: True, it can be a very effective tool, particularly in the rural areas of our nation. Oh, I think our time is almost over. So, we may conclude the discussion, inferring that in order to prevent female foeticide and girl child abandonment, we need to punish the culprits, reward the informers and create awareness in the society.

Preeti: Well said.

[What else could have been said: Though the meaning of this topic is not a complicated one, someone could have explained the term 'female foeticide'. Also, it could have been mentioned in what pitiful condition the abandoned girl children are found. They could also have discussed the mental turmoil of the parents who abandon a girl.**]**

> ***[Performance Analysis:*** *As you might have noticed, many good speakers have participated in this discussion, so it's going to be a tough decision for the evaluators. But as I said, they may decide to send ahead as many candidates as they like, because the PI barrier is still remaining.*

Preeti, the first speaker, spoke fluently and was able to put forth her opinion nicely. Same can be said about Richa, Deepak, Abhinav and Ankita. They all acted professionally, utilized their specialized knowledge in the discussion, avoided unfruitful conflicts, and tackled personal attacks professionally. Richa was the first one to provide the relevant data. Deepak helped bring the discussion back on track when it was about to get derailed. Abhinav handled a personal attack professionally and provided some nice suggestions. Ankita was even able to relate her real life experience to the discussion, which is, by all means, a plus point. All these candidates deserve to be promoted to the next round, i.e., Personal Interview.

Vijay, of course, will not see the next round because he acted as a spoiler. What about Rohan? Even he did nothing more than contradicting what Vijay had said (and that too not so nicely), therefore he won't be promoted to the next round. Vinod has committed the cardinal sin of not adding to the discussion, therefore, he loses his chance.

Please note that more than half of the participants in this discussion were selected for the PI. Don't be surprised if that happens, because the aim of the GD is not to fail the deserving candidates, but to stop the non-deserving ones. That's why you should love a GD.]

[DISCUSSION II]

(A B-School has shortlisted a few students for the Group Discussion process. Since a large number of students were able to cross the cut-off set by them, there are lots of students in the campus. This has compelled the school to fasten the process of discussion. They have decided to call the students in groups of eight, and they can't allow each group to discuss for more than ten minutes. The students are tensed because they have to perform under time pressure, though the evaluators are relaxed because this is not the first time they are facing such a situation. They are professionals with years of experience and can judge the students within limited time, so the students need not worry about that.)

[**Note:** We are taking a highly-tensed situation here. Don't worry, such situations seldom arise; and whenever they do, the mantra for them is well-known: Prepare for the worst and hope for the best.]

Evaluator *(to a group of eight students)*: Dear students, your topic is **'FDI in India'**. There's no need to introduce yourself, as we have a list with your names and photos. You may begin as soon as you are ready. Your time starts now.

Mohit *(takes the opportunity right away)*: Friends, let's understand what FDI is. FDI stands for Foreign Direct Investment, or the investments made by foreign companies and individuals in India. These days a lot is being said about FDI because while many multinational companies want to make investments in India, some people in our politics do not think it will be in our national interest to allow them to do so. Therefore, some political parties are in favour while others are opposing it. We may also...

Raj *(interrupts Mohit tactfully)*: With your permission, I'd like to make a clarification on this point, my friend. FDI must not be confused with FII, i.e., Foreign Institutional Investors, which is, in layman's terms, the foreign financial institutions which invest in the Indian stock markets. Various mutual fund companies, insurance companies, trusts, banks, etc. come in the FII category. While FDI is crucial for our nation's development, as it has been in China, FII is not that crucial because it can be taken away anytime the institutions see more potential in other international markets.

Vinay *(not knowing much about the given topic)*: Could you please elaborate upon that?

Raj: Oh, sure!

Yogita *(interrupts Raj in a composed manner)*: Forgive me, but please allow me this opportunity. While the impact of FDI could be clearly seen in the form of infrastructure, facilities and jobs created by the foreign companies in India, FII money usually refers to the money invested by foreign institutions in our stock markets, securities and bonds, and usually causes our stock indices, like BSE Sensex or NSE Nifty to shoot up in a short time. It means that FDI is a more permanent investment made by the companies, while FII is, more often than not, a temporary investment.

Vinay: Oh, well, that explains it. So, we can say that we must long for FDI more than for FII, because most of the development we see in our urban and industrial areas is a large part due to FDI. But there's another question we must try to answer. What makes our country so attractive a destination for the foreign investors? Would anybody like to answer please?

Ashwini: Sure, and thanks for the opportunity. As we all know, India has a large number of educated people who are ready to work at wages much lower than their European and American counterparts. India is one of the fastest growing economies of the world. We have three sides of our country surrounded with the ocean, which creates a tremendous capability for shipping and sea trade. We have a very reliable banking system which has proved itself even during the recent recession. Moreover, our purchasing power is growing every year and our industrialists have created world class businesses, which have even acquired some international companies. For instance, Hindalco acquired Novelis, Mr Lakshmi Mittal acquired Arcelor, and Tata Motors bought Jaguar and Land Rover operations of Ford. These are just some examples where...

Ramesh: *(Interrupting in between)* And then we cannot forget the contributions made by Non-Residing Indians in directing the investments towards our country, you know while...a... *(forgets his point due to nervousness and situational pressure. He now repents why he had not put more hours in practice.)*

Suresh: I think we have only discussed the positive side of FDI so far. Why do we forget that FDI has also caused a lot of hue and cry? Why is it opposed if it's all good?

Raj: I think you are talking about the current FDI in the retail row; the point one of our friends was about to raise. The thing is that some people believe that entry of huge foreign retailers, such as Wal-Mart, Carrefour, Home Depot, etc. may deprive the local retailers and brands of their customers, because big retailers can afford to lower their prices because of the bulk-purchasing advantage. And if that happens, people working in the unorganized retail sector may lose their jobs and incomes. Whether this apprehension is baseless or not, depends on how prepared our local retailers and brands are for a tough competition.

Yogita: I think FDI in retail also creates jobs if it takes away some. In fact, around 12% of all the manufacturing sector jobs in the US have been created due to FDI. Therefore, we cannot just blame FDI for unemployment problems, though we need to take each step carefully while allowing FDI. However, small retailers can provide customised services to the customers, and they also have nice, family-like relations with many customers. They can compete with big retailers.

Ashwini: I quite agree with you on this. So many new jobs are created when a company sets up its stores and facilities in India. For instance, the supermarkets employ thousands of people in India. The BPOs of foreign companies have employed lakhs of Indians in cities like Bangalore, Mumbai, Pune and Gurgaon. While talking about the cautions we need to take with FDI, I think our governments have done a wise job by not allowing FDI in some sectors, such as Atomic Energy, Arms and ammunition, Railway and mining of metals, because we may need more time to prepare before we allow FDI in these sensitive sectors.

Kanta: Hey, let me speak too! I just want to say that... *(The timer rings.)*

Evaluator: I'm sorry dear, but the time is over. Next batch is waiting already. Thank you everyone!

[What else could have been discussed: What steps could be taken to attract more FDI (Some of them being: improving basic infrastructure – roads, transport, power supply, telecommunication and postal services, etc., strengthening law and order, providing security to the foreigners in India, creating more SEZs, improving logistics facilities, offering concessions to those investors who invest in the semi-urban areas); countries that have made major direct investments in India (Singapore, the UK, Mauritius and the USA being the top ones so far); which sectors the FDI is coming into (IT, telecom, services, real estate, power, health, hotel industry, etc.)]

[Performance Analysis: *As we can see here, perhaps no candidate got a chance to say everything they wanted to. Time pressure may upset those who are not prepared for it, though there are some people who can maintain their composure in the toughest situations.*

Mohit was the first one to speak, and he explained the meaning of FDI in an understandable manner, but he could not make any more significant points (except mentioning a current issue), so he may not be selected for the PI. Raj entered the discussion in the second place and he made his points nicely. His contribution is significant and he will be selected for the next round. Yogita interrupted Raj in a polite manner and was able to make some good points throughout the discussion, so she will be selected for the next round, though she didn't speak much. Vinay didn't know much about the topic; nevertheless, he asked some relevant questions. But that may not be sufficient to take him to the next round. It will depend on the evaluators whether they would like to give him another chance. Ashwini wasn't among the first speakers, but she entered the discussion as soon as she got an opportunity. She made some very nice points and provided good examples to support them, so she will proceed to the PI round. Ramesh and Suresh have not made any significant contributions, though they tried to speak. Kanta didn't get a chance, or we can say, she didn't try enough.]

[DISCUSSION III]

(A multinational banking organization had invited twenty students from various B-Schools for group discussion. These students were shortlisted on the basis of a written test conducted by the organization. Only thirteen students have appeared at the venue. The organizers call them inside the meeting room where the discussion is to take place. Attendance was taken and the students were assigned seats, tags bearing their names placed in front of the seats. They take seats accordingly. While the students were expecting to get a financial topic, a surprise was waiting for them...)

Evaluator: Dear all, I'd like to congratulate you for passing the written test! Today you're here for the second round of our selection procedure – the group discussion. And the topic you will be discussing is... *(removes a chit from a box and reads out...)* **'Success is Money'**. You have twenty minutes to discuss. You may start after two minutes.

(Some students have been stumped while some confident ones start writing points on the pieces of paper provided to them. Two of the students decide to play oversmart, assuming that a banker can see nothing but money. After two minutes, one student takes the initiative...)

Kavita *(a bit nervously)***:** Good morning friends! My name is Kavita and I don't fully agree with the topic. Wealth one possesses is only one measure of one's success, but it's not the only thing that determines the success of a person. Success is measured on various parameters, such as health, good relationship, name, etc. I think we need to discuss them in...

Ajit *(one of the two of our oversmart participants)***:** Sorry to interrupt you ma'am, but I think you are being a bit impractical by saying that success is anything other than money. I mean, tell me one thing that money can't buy? You may talk about love and relationship and all, but none of them will be there if there's no money. Money can buy you any luxury you want, just anything! You may not be able to spend time with your family, but you can see them from your office if you have the video conferencing facilities installed at your home. You can take your family on a grand vacation at the end of the year to compensate for the loss of time you could have spent together! And who doesn't like nice, expensive gifts?

Rohan *(our second oversmart candidate jumps in instantly)***:** I fully agree with my friend Ajit. After all, we are participating in a discussion organized by a financial organization; and speaking against money is not a wise thing to do if you want to sell financial products to the people. Money is the ultimate parameter of success. Unless you are financially successful, nobody respects you anywhere. Just look around and you'll realize that money rules everywhere. May be love, health and relationships play a part in a happy life, still money is above them all. I will say that money is success.

(The evaluator is looking surprised at the unexpected turn the discussion has taken, but he says nothing. Kavita, being a bit under-confident participant, doesn't contradict them immediately, though she should have.)

Suman: I beg to differ from the previous two speakers, because there are many things that matter in life. I don't underestimate the value of money, but I strongly support the point our friend Kavita was trying to make. Money is just one parameter to measure the success of a person, but there are other parameters as well. There have been the people who were extremely rich but still unsuccessful because they never lived happily. On the other hand, there have been people like Mahatma Gandhi, Nelson Mandela and Subhash Chandra Bose, who could have lived luxurious and affluent lives but they gave them up for a higher purpose. We call them successful not because of their wealth, but for what they achieved for the society. Therefore, the topic 'Success is money' is only partially correct.

Kavita *(now sounding confident)***:** Thanks for the support, Suman. I was trying to make a similar point. Many people believe that money is everything. They give up all the pleasures of life in pursuit of it. They think they can buy happiness for their families, but they realize the truth only after the irreparable damage has been done. They may even lose the love of their family members, their health, everything, before they have amassed the wealth they want. Then, they realise their mistake of not giving sufficient time to their own people.

Vishwas: I too believe that money is a medium, not the ultimate success itself. I tend to agree with Kavita and Suman on this point. What is the use of having a great bank balance if it will all be spent in paying doctors' fees? What if no one in the society likes you? What is the use of having a lot of money but no one to enjoy it with?

I think the most misguided people are those who have money but don't know how to use it. Instead of investing it or spending it for a good purpose, they misuse it to create problems for themselves and for the society. For instance, people may develop unhealthy habits, such as drinking, buying super-bikes to race on the roads, spending extravagantly to satiate the hunger of their 'good weather' friends, and in the end, when they have used up all their money, they adopt unlawful methods to fulfil their wishes. In my opinion, that is the worst possible kind of life. Can we call such people successful?

Akshit: No, we definitely can't. I think what a person needs to be called truly successful is a balanced life. I'd say that if a person can reach his life-goals, fulfil the needs and demands of his family, make sufficient money, spend time with his family, and can do something meaningful for the society, he or she can be called successful. It's okay to fall behind in some of these areas because no one can have a perfect life, but he must not totally miss any of them. Why do people get divorced or develop lifestyle diseases? Because they forget their priorities in life. A businessman who doesn't have time for his family, or a father who can't pay his children's school fees, are both behind the mark of success.

Farooq: My friends, I think we should not forget a very important measure of success – how much a person has endured to reach where he has reached. Some people are born with a silver spoon, while some people are born in slums. We can hardly expect both kind of people to get same social and economic atmosphere to get ahead in life. Life throws different kinds of challenges to them. I believe, and I hope you will also agree with me, that if a boy born in a family facing extreme poverty becomes a doctor, he can be called more successful than a businessman's only son who spent all of his father's hard-earned money in living a lavish life.

Vineeta: I agree with Akshit and Farooq. Life is not all about money. Well... that's it.

Swati: Friends, allow me to share some examples with you to prove that success is not all about money. My first example will be the world's richest man, John D. Rockefeller. There was a time when he had unbelievable amounts of money, but he was called a successful man only when he began spending his money for the welfare of the society. Earlier, many people hated him for his merciless acquisition strategies; later on, he was loved by the people when he did charity work. Swami Vivekananda can hardly be counted among rich men, but he was one of the most successful scholars of our country because he established the relevance of ancient Indian knowledge in the world. Similarly, Dr. A.P.J. Abdul Kalam isn't in the list of the richest persons of India, but he is definitely one of the most respected and successful ones. Mother Teresa is another wonderful example. What I want to say is that success has many faces.

Vineeta: Very nice examples, Swati.

Ajit: I think some of our friends are totally rejecting the importance of money here. But let me make it clear that their lofty speeches had no effect on me. Money is almost everything, if not all. Haven't you read about the lives of the rich people? Can't you imagine the luxury of spending time on a five-star cruise liner? Isn't business class of a plane superior to the economy class?

Akshit: My friend, Mr. Ajim Premji and Mr. Narayana Murthy have both been spotted travelling in the economy class and using budget hotels to stay. They have billions, but they are also down to earth. I think these examples are sufficient to prove that luxury is not success.

Rohan: I think I have now realized that money is not the only measure of success.

Mihir: I feel that health of a person is real success. A healthy person can enjoy the life despite any challenges. Then comes relationship. A person, who has the support of others, can fight any battle. And, of course, money is important, to buy all we need.

Suman: Although there's no need to talk about how important money is, yet I'd like to add a few examples. Millions of lives could have been saved if we had sufficient money to feed all the Indians. Many patients can't get treatments because they have no money. Many worthy students give up their dreams of higher education because their families can't bear the expenses. All this can be averted if...

Ajit *(interrupts)*: See, now you are only supporting my views!

Suman *(confidently)*: No, I'm not. I'm only speaking about the value of money, and I think none of us is naive enough to undermine the importance of money.

Evaluator: Sorry people, the time's over. Although I shouldn't, but I'd like to mention here that even the bank employees are human beings. Money matters a lot to us, but true success is not all about money. Well, your results will be declared within half an hour. Till then, you can have a cup of coffee in our canteen. Thank you!

(Ajit knows his result, so he leaves immediately, which may be another foolish step taken by him because a true candidate has patience.)

[**What else could have been discussed:** Success has different meaning to different people. To an artist, success may mean appreciation of his works by the people; to a social worker, success may mean getting justice for weak people of the society; to a common man, success may mean living a calm and prosperous life. They could have also discussed how a person should use his money to reach his goals.]

***[Performance analysis:** Kavita gave a nervous start to the discussion, which is not a good sign for her. Although she tried to make a comeback, yet we can't be absolutely sure if she'll proceed to the next round. Ajit spoke confidently, but whatever he spoke was based on a misguided assumption that people working in a banking organization will not want to hear about the limitations of money (Don't be surprised if you meet some oversmart people* *during a discussion; they do exist!). His views were rejected by the rest of the group, and he will be dropped. Rohan changed his mind very late. Moreover, it's not a good thing to do during a discussion because it implies that you lack confidence and firmness. It's best to choose your side carefully. Suman was the first one to take a firm stand on her views, and she defended her views well. Moreover, she was able to see both the sides of the coin. She will be selected for sure. Vishwas raised some relevant questions and made nice arguments. He will be selected. Akshit talked about the parameters to measure the success of a person. His participation was significant. He also provided some real-life examples. He will be selected. Although Farooq spoke less, yet he made a very valid point that we should not forget the circumstances of the people while measuring their success. He has displayed high levels of maturity, and he will get selected. Vineeta didn't provide enough input to get selected. Swati has provided some very nice examples, and she has qualified for the next round. Mihir didn't add anything new. He will be dropped. Those candidates who couldn't open their mouths will be rejected straightaway.]*

❑❑❑

10

Some Important Topics

1. Globalisation

In today's world, no country can afford to stay isolated. All the nations are interdependent. When the citizens of various nations interact with each other for business and other purposes, they work towards global integration. Information, finances, products and services, even the cultural features of different societies are carried across the globe. This process is commonly called globalisation. In short, globalisation means global integration. It couldn't have been possible without the development of communication, transport, media and global trade. One of the earliest examples of globalisation is the 'Silk route', which was spread in three continents – Asia, Europe and Africa. Let's see how globalisation affects India.

Pros:

1. It helps strengthen relations with other countries. (A country, which has investments in some other country, will definitely want peaceful relations with that country.) India now has strategic partnerships with many nations.

2. Many multinationals have set up their operations in India. They not only invest heavy amounts, but also provide jobs to millions of Indian people. This helps in the economic development of our nation. Moreover, the MNCs pay comparatively higher salaries to their employees.

3. Many Indian companies have also set up their operations in other countries. By doing so, they get a strategic advantage over their competitors, as they get required raw material and/or services from the countries which provide them at lower costs. Moreover, they spread the influence of our nation in the world.

4. India can also import essential technology from other countries. It will help in the technological progress of the nation.

5. When people from different nations interact with each other, they learn positive aspects of other cultures. They acquire new ideas. This helps in intellectual development of people.

6. Due to globalisation, world class facilities are created in the country itself. Many cities like Delhi, Gurgaon, Bangalore, Pune, etc. have world class hospitals, educational institutes, office buildings, etc. because the MNCs have set up their offices there. The development of Singapore, Taiwan and Hong-Kong is also due to globalisation.

Cons:

1. The entry of foreign companies may be a threat to the Indian companies, especially, the small and medium industries. The MNCs usually have bulk-purchasing and supply-chain advantages over small companies (because they can import from wherever they get the cheapest raw material, and since they buy huge quantities, they get concessions). People lose jobs when a company is closed down due to the intense competition from the MNCs.

2. When the Indian companies import from abroad, they create jobs into those countries, while they could do that in India. (For instance, an Indian company, which imports readymade T-shirts from Sri Lanka or Bangladesh, creates jobs for the manufacturers of those countries.) It's just what the MNCs do when they come here.

3. The influence of other cultures may bring about the changes which may be against the Indian culture. There may be the things which are fully acceptable in the other cultures but not considered appropriate in our country. This may lead to the clash of cultures.

4. People buy foreign brands, sometimes just under the influence of advertising (and the MNCs have huge budgets for the advertisement of their products). This means loss of customers for the Indian companies.

Our suggestion: While the process of globalisation is inevitable, we need to stay prepared for the challenges it poses to us. Concrete steps are needed to be taken to prepare the Indian companies for these challenges. India should wisely negotiate its demands in the world's trade forums and organisations. Steps should be taken to ensure that our country reaps full benefits of our enormous skilled manpower advantage (as we are doing in the BPO industry). Interests of our small and medium enterprises should be protected. Their productivity and efficiency need to be improved before they can take up the challenges of the world.

In short, we need to make sure that we reap maximum benefits of globalisation.

2. Global Warming

Rise in temperature of the atmosphere is called global warming. It has been noted that earth's atmospheric temperature has been rising at a rate faster than it used to happen a century ago. This means that the human activities have fastened the process of global warming. Deforestation, emissions from factories, automobiles and power plants and burning of fossil fuels (petrol, diesel, coal, etc. due to any reason) cause an increase in the levels of carbon dioxide in our atmosphere. Carbon dioxide retains solar heat into the atmosphere (greenhouse effect) and this causes atmospheric temperature to rise. Besides, there are natural causes of global warming, which add to the problem. Global warming was noted back in the colonial era, when the industrial revolution was taking place in England, but it didn't become a major issue until recently. In December, 1997, the representatives of various countries gathered in Kyoto (Japan). They negotiated and signed an agreement to cut the emission of carbon dioxide and other greenhouse gases. This is known as Kyoto Protocol. The biggest contributors to global warming were identified to be the USA, China, Canada, etc., while India has also been added to the list.

Effects of global warming:

1. Global warming causes melting of ice at the earth's poles. This causes a rise in the sea-level across the globe. This rise, if not controlled, may endanger the cities which are located near the sea (New York, Mumbai, Dubai, etc.). Some of them may submerge in the water completely. Maldives, an entire country, is facing the grave danger of submerging in the ocean due to global warming.

2. Global warming may muddle with the balance of various ecosystems. Some of the animal and plant species in some regions have suffered greatly due to rise in temperature. Some species have been so badly affected that they are facing the danger of extinction. Similarly, some animal species have been forced to leave their natural habitats and move to the cooler parts of the world.

3. Rise in the atmospheric temperature causes more rainfall in some regions (which may cause floods in those areas) and less in others (which may cause drought in those areas). Some parts of the world will face the dangers of floods, hurricanes and sea storms, while some others may turn into deserts due to global warming.

What can be done to stop global warming:

1. Firstly, we should create awareness about global warming. When people come to know more about its effects, they will do more

to stop it. When more and more people know about it, only then the desired success may come to us. TV and radio channels, newspapers and magazines must highlight the issue as much as possible. NGOs can (and do) play an important role in creating awareness.

2. Planting more trees helps reduce the levels of carbon dioxide in the atmosphere, because trees consume carbon dioxide and emit oxygen. This may be the single most important countermeasure we can take.

3. Governments of various nations must strictly enforce the pollution control laws on the factories and automobiles which release huge amounts of carbon dioxide in the atmosphere. Harmful waste products from the factories must be disposed in an effective and safest way possible.

4. People should learn to recycle the waste products. Use of reusable and recyclable materials must be encouraged. It will ease pressure on factories to produce more.

5. Air conditioning and heating appliances must not be overused, as they generate and release heat in the atmosphere. The same applies on water heaters.

6. Whenever possible, people should use public transport instead of own automobiles.

7. Reducing consumption of electricity may help reduce the global warming. The less we use, the less they'll generate.

3. AIDS

AIDS stands for **A**cquired **I**mmuno **D**eficiency **S**yndrome. It is a disease of immune system. A person with AIDS is vulnerable to the diseases and infections which may not harm a healthy individual. These infections and diseases often prove fatal to the AIDS patients. AIDS is caused by HIV (Human Immuno Deficiency Virus). It is a transmittable disease. It is also an incurable disease so far; therefore, it is best to prevent AIDS.

HIV virus transmits:

1. By having sex with an infected person.
2. Through infected needles.
3. When infected blood is accidentally donated to other people.
4. From the infected mothers to their babies during pregnancy or through breast-feeding.

What can be done to prevent AIDS:

1. Creating awareness is extremely important to fight AIDS. Many people don't know about AIDS, its effects, and transmission, therefore, they carelessly indulge in unsafe sexual activities. This must be stopped. Moreover, the individuals with AIDS must be identified and provided the best possible treatments. This will not be accomplished if the society doesn't stop discriminating against people with AIDS, because discrimination stops people from admitting their condition. The AIDS patients must be given proper respect.
2. Having sex with multiple partners increases the chances of acquiring AIDS. Therefore, staying loyal to one's life-partner may be an effective preventive step. Using condoms may also reduce the risk up to an extent.
3. Hospitals must have proper facilities to test donated blood (and organs) to prevent HIV.
4. Using disposable injection needles, which are broken after one use, is one way of preventing the HIV infection.
5. If an HIV-infected pregnant lady takes proper treatment, she may reduce the chances of transmitting AIDS to the baby.

6. People who have engaged in unsafe sexual activities or drug-addiction (where drugs are injected into the body using needles) should get tested for HIV.

Our suggestion: AIDS is the enemy of the society. Knowledge can be our greatest weapon against this enemy. We should take all the possible steps to prevent the spread of AIDS. We should also invest more in research about AIDS so that we can prepare an effective medicine to cure it.

4. Science – Boon or Bane?

In favour:

1. Without science, we would still be living in the dark times. Scientific discoveries and inventions (satellites, rockets, etc.) enabled us discover our world and the universe.

2. Medical sciences have developed so many drugs, vaccinations and therapies for treatment and prevention of various common as well as lethal diseases, which have helped human race a lot. They have saved lives! Everything from Polio drops, ventilators, X-Rays and heart transplant facilities to common cold medicine and pain-killers is an invention of science.

3. Electricity, a magnificent gift of science, helps us everyday, in every walk of life. Electric gadgets, machines and equipment (TV, AC, Refrigerator, washing machine and all) have, beyond any doubt, made our lives easy.

4. Science has made this vast world a global village by enabling us travel faster (using planes, ships, trains, etc.) and communicate instantly (using phone, internet, telegrams, etc.). Cars, scooters and motorbikes are all scientific inventions. Even the use of fuels, such as Petrol, Diesel and CNG has been possible due to science.

5. Harnessing nuclear power has provided us an efficient and powerful fuel. Nuclear radiations are also used in the treatment of cancer.

6. Fertilizers, tractors and electric pumps have made it possible to produce sufficient foodgrains to meet our nation's requirements. Genetically modified foods may become a better source of nutrition in the future (after sufficient testing has been done.)
7. Even the ancient Ayurvedic medicines come in the sphere of science. Therefore, we can say that science has always been a part of Indian culture.

You can say as much as you like to in favour of science. You can use the examples from the room your GD is taking place in.

Against:

1. Science has fastened the pace of human progress and this may be against the rules of nature. We live in a fast, restless world. Lifestyle diseases such as high blood pressure, obesity, depression, etc. are mainly because of the unnatural and comfortable lifestyle, which science has made possible.
2. Nuclear power is also being used for destructive purposes (Hiroshima and Nagasaki attacks being such example). Also, nuclear disasters may take thousands of lives within minutes; therefore, they are dangers for all forms of life (Chernobyl plant disaster, Fukushima nuclear plant disaster.)
3. Internet provides a faster mean of communication, but it also creates distances between the people. When there was no social networking, people used to meet or handwrite to each other more frequently. In a way, people have cut-off from each other, thanks to science.
4. Genetically modified foods may prove to be unhealthy in future. They may create the health complications we can't even imagine right now.
5. Mobile phones interfere with the personal moments of the people. You just can't put it away or switch it off. You can't even sleep without the fear of missing an important call.

Our suggestion: *(We advise you to speak in favour of science, because the advantages of science clearly outweigh the disadvantages. Though you may mention some of the disadvantages listed above to prove that you have seen both the sides of the coin. However, you should stick to your original stand till the end of the discussion.)*

5. Euthanasia (Mercy Killing)

In favour:

1. To end the endless sufferings of a person, euthanasia should be allowed, at least in the rarest of the rare cases. There have been the cases when a merciful death became better than the agonizing life of a patient.

2. Sometimes, the families of the patients find themselves unable to bear the burden of the expenses of hospitals and medicines. They might need to sell their houses and belongings too. Since the government can't provide financial help to every such family, euthanasia should be allowed if there are no chances of recovery of a patient. Moreover, the hospitals of our country usually face a dearth of healthcare facilities, like beds, machines, etc. Why not provide other serious patients (who may have better chances to live) the facilities which this unfortunate patient is using?

3. Some patients cannot even speak while suffering from an excruciating pain. Therefore, their immediate family members must be allowed to speak on their behalf, and the patients should be allowed a painless death if the family members suggest so.

4. In some of the most unfortunate cases, even if a patient's life is saved, still it will be a life full of misery and pain (such as, in the cases of full body paralysis and continuous and everlasting acute pain). If such patients (or their families) plea for a merciful death, they may be allowed to go ahead. After all, a person is the owner of his own life, and we should not deny anyone this right.

Against:

1. Euthanasia may discourage a lot of people who are fighting similar severe problems, and, hence, it may drive the society towards despair and depression. Other such patients, who have fought on so far, may also demand similar painless death.

2. Since only God can give a life, we have no right to take it away under any circumstances *(Same point can be made while speaking on Capital punishment or suicide).*

3. May be the patient, who can't speak or react, wants to live on! How can we know what he/she wants?

4. Some patients make a miraculous recovery in the moments when all seems dark. Why deprive a patient of such chances?

5. One life's loss is a loss for that person's entire family. When a person dies, his entire family suffers. Therefore, he alone must not be allowed to take the decision about ending his own life.

6. It would indicate a victory of disease over human determination; therefore, it must not be allowed.

Our suggestion: You may speak either in favour of or against euthanasia, but before you declare your conclusion, you must show that you have considered the points made by those against your viewpoint. Play safe and wise, but also prove your ability to take decisions. *(Read about the 'Aruna Shanbaug case' over the internet. This case is so important because the victim suffered in a vegetative state for decades, and the Supreme Court gave an exceptional decision of 'passive euthanasia' in this case. You can use the example in GD.)*

6. Capital Punishment (Death Penalty)

In favour:

1. It should not be abolished because it acts as a deterrent against crime. People fear death, hence, they don't commit severe crimes due to fear of capital punishment.

2. Hardcore criminals have no place in a civilized society. There's no harm in hanging them, because they will commit more crimes if they lived.
3. A murdered person's family must get justice. Therefore, capital punishment must be awarded to murderers and rapists, at least in rare cases. Tit for tat.
4. Some hardcore criminals get out of jail because they have strong political connections. Some criminals have been found running their syndicates from jails. Sometimes, the terrorists kidnap people or hijack planes and demand the release of the captive terrorists (as in IC-814 case, in which a plane was hijacked and the government had to bargain with the terrorists to get the citizens back). Why not hang such criminals and end their fear forever?
5. Even some of the most advanced countries (like USA) use capital punishment as a tool for justice.

Against:

1. Since we can't give a dead person life, we have no right to take life of anyone.
2. Even though we have had capital punishment since ages now, crimes are still taking place. In fact, the crime rate is growing in many areas. How is it effective then?
3. Even the hardcore criminals must be given at least one chance to reform. May be they can lead a good social life afterwards!
4. Many countries, which don't award capital punishment, see it as a barbaric way of providing justice. Therefore, capital punishment spoils the image of our nation.
5. Morally it is not right to take a life. It also casts bad impression on the children.

Our suggestion: You may conclude by adding that capital punishment should only be awarded in the rarest of the rare cases, but it should not be abolished altogether. It is another tool of justice and should be used patiently. (Many experts believe that in some countries, it is misused. For instance, some governments use capital punishment to crush the opposition, or to kill a whistle-blower. Cases have been reported from Iraq, China and some other countries, and human right activists have raised voices against it.)

7. Reservation in Jobs/Education

In favour:

1. To uplift those people who were forced to live second grade social and economic lives for centuries (SC, ST, OBC), reservations are necessary. It is important for the overall development of the nation that every caste participates in it.

2. Reservation is essential to bring social and educational equality in society. It helps the backward castes to emerge in the society and gain a respectable place.

3. By creating equality in society, reservation helps strengthen the unity of India.

4. Some wise people, who prepared our constitution, created provision for reservation. We should not challenge their wisdom.

5. According to some surveys, even now a very high percentage of higher posts in the government jobs is occupied by the general category people, who are fewer in number than the people belonging to the backward castes. It is essential to provide reservation to end this unevenness.

6. Moreover, the backward castes still face social discrimination in some areas of the nation.

Against:

1. Reservation is against the concept of equal opportunity which our constitution emphasises on. Even the humanity calls for

equal opportunity to everyone. Besides, many social groups and communities across the globe complain that they were discriminated against for a long time, but most of the countries do not provide reservations to such groups. Why should India be an exception?

2. Even socially and economically strong people are enjoying reservation in the name of caste. Reservation may be on economic basis, but caste-based reservation is not fair.

3. Reservation has been there for more than half a century, and it has not helped the society much, as backward classes have not benefitted much from it. They still live in a poor and dreadful condition and a lot needs to be done for them. Reservation has just become a tool of vote bank politics. Its original objective has not been fulfilled.

4. Instead of uniting people, reservation creates differences between them. People get divided when they see certain castes enjoying special benefits.

5. Reservation kills merit. Wouldn't it be better to provide better education to the underprivileged ones up to the high school level, so that they can compete with others? Will nation's development not be affected if we do not give preference to merit?

6. Many seats reserved for SC, ST and OBC stay vacant every year. Why not make them general category seats, so that such wastage could be stopped?

7. If the backward classes still face discrimination, it means that the reservation has failed to fulfil its very purpose! Why continue it then?

Our suggestion: You may speak either in favour of or against reservation, but don't forget to add that it should be there only for a limited time, not indefinitely. Also, provide relevant examples to support your viewpoint.

8. Co-education

In favour:

1. Co-education breaks the mental barrier of shyness, which otherwise boys and girls may feel in each others' presence. It enhances the chances that the members of both the sexes will be able to work with each other (which they usually have to once they're in a job). It definitely makes people open-minded and more confident. People who never had co-education may find it difficult to work with the individuals of opposite sex.

2. It enables both the sexes understand each other's qualities and requirements. It may prove to be an extremely valuable lesson in the future, even while making the most crucial decisions (such as marriage).

3. When boys and girls communicate freely, they learn from each other. They improve their social and communication skills. It's an established fact.

4. In the western countries, there's co-education in almost every institute. Therefore, a person who has never had an experience of studying or working in the presence of other sex, may find it difficult to adjust in those conditions. They may not pursue their studies and careers comfortably in the West.

Against:

1. Students often take admission into co-education institutions for wrong reasons. Many of them just like love affairs, or to simply waste time in each other's presence, which is against the very idea of education itself.

Our suggestion: Don't speak against co-education, or you may be labelled as a person, who is 'unable to work or study in the presence of the opposite sex'. Support co-education, no matter what your personal beliefs are.

9. Love Marriages and Arranged Marriages

In favour of love marriages:

1. Love marriage may be a more rational decision because the couple knows each other before the marriage. Love helps them understand each-other's true nature. It may solve many post-marital problems.

2. Love, no doubt, strengthens the bond of marriage too. A loving couple will not divorce each other for petty reasons. In fact, no marriage can survive for long without love. Some people argue that love can develop even after the marriage; but what if it doesn't? What if the life partners can't tolerate each other? Why take a chance?

3. A couple who did love marriage cannot shed the accountability on others should the marriage fail. They are responsible for their own choices. In the arranged marriage, it becomes *'parents' fault'*.

4. Even the love marriage can be arranged! Parents are not always against love marriages.

5. Love does not recognize the boundaries of caste and religion. People who love each other may even do inter-religion or inter-caste marriage. Therefore, in a way, love marriages liberate the society from some baseless and divisive traditions.

In favour of arranged marriages:

1. When the elders arrange a marriage, they use their invaluable life experience to make right partner choices for their children. It may be a crucial factor in the stability of the marriage.

2. There's hardly any data suggesting that love marriages last longer than the arranged ones.

3. Since the members of a society whole-heartedly support an arranged marriage (at least in our country), they may also provide invaluable support to the couple if any issues arise after

the marriage. A couple who has done love marriage may or may not get such support from the society.

4. Loving couple may overlook each-other's faults, and this 'accepted blindness towards each-other's faults' may prove devastating once they have married and shared responsibilities as husband and wife. They may not find each other suitable anymore.

5. Love can happen after the marriage too! Who says people whose marriages are arranged do not love each other?

Our suggestion: You may either support love marriage or arranged marriage, but you should appreciate the rational points made by those who don't support your views. An examiner may have a viewpoint different than yours.

10. Nuclear Power: A Gift or a Curse?

In favour:

1. Nuclear power is a long-lasting and more powerful source of energy when compared with other sources. Even a small amount of nuclear material can generate enough power to meet the demands of a metro city or a nuclear powered submarine for a long time.

2. Nuclear power helps preserve traditional energy resources (coal, petroleum) and provides a powerful alternative to them.

3. It has been successfully adopted as a primary source of power in many developed countries. Why should we not take advantage of it? Especially when we have to import a lot of crude oil at high prices?

4. Nuclear power is a clean power. Very little amount of pollutants is produced by nuclear power plants, while thermal power plants release a large amount of carbon and other pollutants in the air.

5. Nuclear power definitely has a lot more potential and scope in the future, and the possibilities are still being researched.

6. Nuclear power is more reliable than wind and solar energy. Sun may not be visible on some days and wind may be too slow to generate enough power, but nuclear power can always be used.

Against:

1. Nuclear power plants may cause devastating accidents, such as the Fukushima and Chernobyl ones.

2. It is very difficult to dump nuclear wastes safely as they emit harmful radiation for a very long time. Working in nuclear power plants may cause health hazards which may not be detected for years.

3. Atom bombs have been the most dreadful weapons of destruction ever used by human kind. Thousands of people died instantly in the Hiroshima and Nagasaki cities, when atom bombs were dropped on them. Nuclear weapons are much more powerful than the bombs used there. They may end the entire life on the earth if used unwisely. Moreover, terrorists may create nuclear weapons and use them against the people!

4. Research and management of nuclear power sources and technology are an expensive affair. Why not spend some amounts on research work on natural power sources (wind, tides, solar power, etc.)? They are far safer than nuclear power, after all!

Our suggestion: If used wisely, nuclear power may definitely be a gift to humanity. Any power may be a curse when used unwisely and for destructive purposes. Therefore, instead of talking against nuclear power, we must learn to use it in a safe and most efficient manner.

11. Social Networking Sites are Harmful to the Society

In favour of the topic:

1. Since the content which is published on the social networking sites cannot be observed all the time, some people post the content absolutely not suitable for children. It may be extremely violent or sexual in nature. Think what kind of impression it will make on children's tender hearts and developing minds! That's the reason why many elders don't even like internet.
2. Terrorists may take advantage of social networking sites by communicating with each other without almost any restriction. All they need to do is create accounts on such sites.
3. Some people post defamatory and offensive content about the people they don't like. They misuse social networking sites. Sometimes, objectionable and often edited photos of girls are posted, which may cause mental agony to the targetted girl. Even the great men are not spared sometimes.
4. Some people publish the content which can hurt the religious sentiments of the people. Such content creates hatred among people, and it may even cause violence and riots.
5. People often waste a lot of time on the social networking sites. Moreover, they hardly meet each other in person if they have met on a social site. This is creating a social isolation.

Against the topic (favouring social networking sites):

1. Social networking sites enable people to come together despite the physical distances between them. Even the shy individuals, who are reluctant to meet people in person, use these sites. Therefore, the social networking sites are uniting the society.
2. People share their problems on these sites. This helps them de-stress. Moreover, they may even get pragmatic (practical) solutions to their problems from other people.

3. Social networking sites have played major roles in uniting the people against injustice and dictatorships in some countries (as during Arab uprisings). This way they provided millions of people a platform where they can demonstrate for their freedom and rights.
4. People make new friends, share ideas, and meet long-separated friends on these sites. People learn a lot from each other over these websites.
5. Since people express their problems and emotions on these sites, social networking sites may even help the society (and police) prevent a person from committing suicide.
6. Social networking sites may help police recognize and catch criminals, because even the criminals use these sites! In fact, they have already helped police reach the criminals in some cases.
7. Since people are too busy in their lives these days, the social networking sites provide a good alternative to meeting each other in person. You may not meet a friend in person, but you can always send a message to him or her.

Our suggestion: Like everything else, social networking too may be used for or against the well-being of the people. It depends on people how they use them. We just cannot ban something which allows people to express themselves; though a little, impartial moderation will not harm anyone.

12. Brain Drain

Brain drain is the process by virtue of which a large number of skilful and talented workers and students leave a country to work (or to get higher education and then work) in abroad. It may be for various reasons – higher salaries, higher education, more opportunities, better lifestyles, etc. There's a good demand for the students passing out from our premier institutes (IITs, IIMs, AIIMS, etc.).

In favour of brain drain:

1. It has been observed that the Indian talent does not get sufficient opportunity and respect in India. A person who has been to abroad suddenly becomes important in our society. There have been the great men and athletes who were little known in India before they proved their mettle in other countries; and when they returned to India, their talent became visible to all. This tendency of our society promotes brain drain.

2. Since we don't have sufficient seats for our students in the premier institutes of our country (moreover, we have very few world class institutes for our huge population), it's quite natural for people to go abroad in search of higher education. After completing their education, they get high salaries in those countries. Who doesn't care for higher salaries? Furthermore, in our country, a lot of seats are reserved on the caste basis. Under such conditions, it becomes a kind of compulsion for many workers and students to go abroad for higher education and/or better work opportunities.

3. Indians abroad not only send money to their families in India, but they also act as social and cultural ambassadors of our country. This helps in the economic development of India and improves India's cultural image abroad. They even contribute to the tourism sector of India. We can clearly see our NRI doctors' impact on the development of health tourism in India. After seeing the Indian doctors performing well in their countries, the foreigners come to India for a quick and cheaper but quality treatment. Brain drain is not all bad!

4. Many NRIs and people of the Indian origin have established big companies abroad (Lakshmi Mittal being one of them). They have created a great name for our nation. Moreover, some of them invest heavily in India. This way they contribute to FDI coming to India.

5. Some NRIs also donate to the NGOs working in India. This way they play their part in promoting the welfare of our society.
6. When we can change jobs for higher pay-checks in our own country, what's wrong with going abroad when we get higher salaries there?
7. Since now we have multinationals in our own country, many of the talented employees and students prefer to stay home instead of going abroad, because they get similar salaries here. Therefore, brain drain is no longer a big problem.
8. India has to participate in the process of globalization; we cannot keep all our talent to ourselves (especially now, when many foreigners are choosing to come to India and work here).

Against:

1. The Indian government spends a lot of money to provide high quality education at the rates affordable to the Indian people. When people study here and then leave to work abroad, the government incurs great financial losses.
2. Many Indians, who had gone abroad years ago, have played crucial role in the development of those countries. Many engineers in the NASA (and the multinational firms like Microsoft) are Indians. So many world class doctors are Indians. Many well-known businessmen are of the Indian origin. If we could have kept our precious talent to ourselves, we could have been a better developed society by now.
3. The students who go to other nations for higher studies also pay hefty tuition fees to the foreign institutes they study in. This way they transfer large sums out of the country.
4. How can people leave their old parents and motherland just in pursuit of wealth and luxury? They should be more patriotic. Money is not the only goal of education. There should be the

people who work for the poor (some of the students who studied in the top institutes have taken this step).

Our suggestion: Since the problem of brain drain seems to be contracting with emergence and entry of the MNCs in India, this problem doesn't seem to be as big any longer as it looked earlier. We should create more educational facilities in India and remove red-tapism and corruption from our country. Above all, we should learn to respect our talent. This will help retain more and more talented people in India.

13. Vegetarianism

India is one of the very few nations where a very large part of the population has adopted vegetarian food habits. In vegetarianism, the diet basically consists of vegetables and foodgrains, and meat is avoided.

In favour:

1. Animals help the human race in many ways. Animals provide us milk and other essential items (wool, oils of therapeutic value, leather, etc.). They are our friends and we should show mercy to them by not killing them just for taste. That's why, the organizations like PETA are now standing against animal-killing.

2. There's always violence involved in killing animals, no matter what the purpose of killing is. We should not support such violence by demanding meat for food purposes.

3. Animals feel pain because they have a nervous system. How can we make them suffer that insufferable agony for our taste? Just because they can't speak our language?

4. Plants can provide almost all the nutrients essential for human survival. Why not rely on plant food then?

5. What right we have to take life if we can't create one?

6. Medical data has established a link between higher number of heart diseases and consumption of meat. Many Western doctors are advising their patients to add more and more vegetables to their diet.

7. Vegetarianism has been a part of the Indian culture for a long time. We must preserve and promote vegetarianism.

Against:

1. There are some essential nutrients which are either not found in vegetarian food, or they are found in traces (Vitamin B_{12} being one). Deficiency of these nutrients can hamper with the development of human brain and the rest of the body. If we don't eat meat, we may have to take multi-vitamins and animal-oil capsules, which again are derived from animals.

2. There are some parts of the world where vegetation cannot grow easily because of extreme temperatures. Some areas are too dry and some are too cold. People have no choice but consume meat in such places. Since anyone might have to work or live in such areas, they must be able to consume meat when they need to.

3. Very few countries in the world have large vegetarian population. Therefore, when a vegetarian person goes abroad to live or to study, he faces difficulty finding vegetarian food; and when it's available, it can be very expensive sometimes.

4. Vegetarianism has been associated with health problems like Arthritis and some immune system problems. To avoid these problems, we need to eat non-veg food.

5. Evidences from ancient scriptures suggest that meat has been a part of the Indian food and medicine since long periods of time. Some of the Ayurvedic books even talk about what meats can be consumed to treat different disorders.

6. If we all adopt completely vegetarian food habits, we will have a danger of running out of required agricultural land soon. Then

we will have to cut a lot of trees for land, which won't be good for the nature.

Our suggestion: Do not rigidly support either vegetarianism or non-vegetarianism. Be flexible in your approach. While you are free to choose whether you want to support veg or non-veg, you should keep in mind that people (including evaluators!) have freedom to choose their own food habits. Moreover, you might have to work in the societies where veg/non-veg is preferred. Support the points you make with suitable examples and scientific data.

14. Multi-tasking

Multi-tasking means carrying out many tasks simultaneously. For instance, talking over mobile while driving, or typing and listening to music simultaneously. Let's see if it's as good as it looks.

In favour:

1. Multi-tasking is the need of the hour. A woman may have to take care of her baby and talk to her friend over the mobile phone simultaneously. Similarly, an employee may have to reply to his boss's e-mail while talking to a customer at the same time. Sometimes, a person may have to do three activities at one time.
2. Multi-tasking saves time. When you accomplish two tasks at one time, you get more time for other activities, or rest.
3. While multi-tasking, people may become ambidextrous (able to use both hands efficiently) over the time (for example, some people can type fast with both the hands). This will help a person develop both hemispheres of brain.
4. Multi-tasking may give others an impression that you are a smart and busy person, as you are handling two or more activities at the same time. (A minor advantage!)

Against:

1. Multi-tasking affects efficiency of a person, and it has been proved scientifically. When you do two or more activities

together, you take more time to complete each one of them, because you're not paying enough attention to either.

2. Multi-tasking lowers the level of awareness of a person. When you manage multiple activities at the same time, you can't pay the required amount of attention to any one of them. After a few weeks, it becomes a habit, and the person tends to give insufficient attention to the tasks in hand. This may lead to the wastage of time.

3. Multi-tasking doesn't let people enjoy any activity to the full extent. For instance, you may not fully enjoy a movie while talking to someone over a phone.

4. Multi-tasking may lead to unnecessary stress. When you manage multiple tasks simultaneously, occurrence of stress is quite natural. Stress is bad not only for health, but also for the awareness level of a person.

5. Multi-tasking is a cause behind many accidents. It has been found in many road accident cases that a person was driving and talking over mobile at the same time when he committed an accident because he couldn't notice the other person. This is why there's a ban on driving and using mobile simultaneously.

6. Multi-tasking may save time in the short run but it may lead to wastage of time in the long run. When you don't do a work properly, you may have to repeat it a number of times. If, unfortunately, it becomes a habit, you repeat every task many times, which may lead to more wastage of time. You may have met the people who don't do the things correctly at first (because they multi-task!) and then repeat the whole process again.

Our suggestion: Multi-tasking may sound good at first, but when it becomes a habit, it takes toll on a person's health, his attention and his awareness. Therefore, it may not be a good idea to do it all the time.

You must give sufficient attention to at least the important activities. Avoid multi-tasking when possible, and do it when necessary. This may be the only practical option available to a person in present times.

15. Effects of Video/Computer Games on Children

In favour:

1. To an extent, video/computer games make a child smart. They compel the child's mind to work fast under tense conditions presented by the game. Also, intelligence games like Chess, Crossword and Mathematical puzzles are available online. They help in the development of a child's brain.

2. A child gets a beforehand experience of the coming life-challenges through these games. For example, through a car-driving game, a child learns certain things about the process of driving. This experience may help him later on when he actually learns driving. In fact, it had been found in one study that the children who play the car-driving games also tend to take up their first driving lessons easy when compared to those who never played such games. No wonder that aviation industry, air force, and even the army uses similar virtual games to train the pilots and the soldiers.

3. Video/computer games make a child learn a great deal about the new technology and the world. For instance, when you play farming games, you may come to know the names of agriculture equipment, vegetables and fruits. You may also learn about the cultures of the nations. You even find the latest technology only available in the most advanced countries.

4. Some computer games (such as Farmville, Cityville, etc.) socially connect people. While playing some games, kids chat with each other, which may improve their communication skills and knowledge.

5. Under friends' pressure, a child may have no choice but to play these games. (Because everyone's playing, so should I!)

Against:

1. Video/computer games lead to wastage of time. Children spend hours and hours on these games. This precious time could be spent on studies, playing outdoor games, and other developmental activities.

2. Video/computer games take a child to a virtual world where he forgets the real world's real challenges. This may affect his precious abilities to face the real world.

3. Some games, especially the war games, are full of violence. A child's amateur mind may get a wrong message from such games. If these games occupy him fully, he may even slightly bend towards violence (it is an established fact that the children learn violent behaviour from games and movies), or, at least, may not be able to see the positive side of life. In this way, these games may take away his ability to appreciate life. They may induce negative thinking.

4. If a child cannot differentiate between real life and game-life, he may commit blunders as a grown up person. For instance, a teenager may drive recklessly (because that's what he has been trained for by his driving game!) and meet an accident. Real life is not like games where we get multiple chances.

5. It may sound incredible to you, but now a new form of addiction has come in the limelight – Addiction to computer/video games. Some children were found to be living away from the real world, spending hours and hours in their rooms every day, playing computer games. Some of them were treated medically for their addictions!

6. Video games, if played for longer durations, may affect the level of awareness of a kid. What more, they affect the eyesight of a kid, because they are played from a short distance!

7. Moreover, these games are very expensive! They may cost a lot to the parents.

Our suggestion: Video/computer games, if played for limited time, may be good for a kid's mental development. But when they claim a good part of a child's time, their negative effects outweigh the positive ones. Therefore, parents must take care that their children take part in outdoor games (which are essential for both physical and mental development of kids) and other constructive activities; and, of course, studies.

16. Great Leaders are Born, Not Trained

In favour:

1. Some of the most influential world leaders are believed to have born with the leadership qualities (Examples: Napoleon, Alexander the Great, etc.).
2. Some of the leadership qualities (such as charisma) cannot be learned. People are born either with or without them.

Against:

1. Most of the great leaders were made, not born (Examples: Mahatma Gandhi, Oprah Winfrey, Dr. A.P.J. Abdul Kalam and Abraham Lincoln, etc.). They became extraordinary by learning from the life.
2. Most of the leadership qualities, such as confidence, integrity, enthusiasm, assertiveness, communication skills, dedication, etc., can be developed through observation, experience, education and training. Anyone can earn them.
3. Even the born leaders had to learn some traits through rigorous training and hardship. They were not born with all the qualities that a leader needs.

4. The view that 'leaders are only born, not made' has been refuted by many medical studies and experiments. It has been proved that leaders can be made.

Our suggestion: Leaders can be made. Leadership qualities can be acquired through training and education. It may be risky for anyone to support the dogmatic view that the leaders are only born.

[**Note:** Same or similar points can be used in the topic 'Managers are born, not made'. Just support your views with examples of great managers (Jack Welch being a great manager as well as a leader).]

17. Work Hard or Work Smart?

In favour of hard work:

1. No great thing has ever been achieved without hard work. All the inventors, athletes, businessmen, writers, toppers and philosophers had to work very hard to achieve what they did.
2. Without hard work, we cannot even fulfil our basic needs. If the farmers don't work hard, we may not get sufficient crops to feed all the people. If our *jawans* don't work hard, we may not be able to defend our borders. If the labour doesn't work hard, we may not live in houses. If the housewives don't work hard, they may not take care of their families. There's no substitution to hard work.
3. A hardworking person is tough. He can get through thick and thin. He may accept the toughest challenges of life.
4. A person, who doesn't work hard, may grow lazy. People prefer a hardworking person over a lazy one.
5. Even in order to learn to work smart, we must work hard.

In favour of smart work:

1. Working smart doesn't necessarily mean avoiding hard work altogether. It means that we can reduce the work pressure by adopting a smarter way. There are the people who work hard

all their lives but achieve nothing or too little, while some smart people get all the cream. They get promotions, they get respect; and they get rich!

2. Even the hard work must be done smartly. It may save time and energy, and reduce unnecessary stress.

3. Unless the direction of hard work is smartly chosen, it may not yield the results we desire.

4. A smart person is also smart enough to earn respect of others.

Our suggestion: Both hard work and smart work are crucial for success. Almost all the great achievers in the world had to work both harder and smarter. A person must be able to work hard whenever he needs to, and act smart whenever there's an opportunity. Smart work cannot be an alternative to hard work, and vice-versa. Both hard work and smart work must be done simultaneously.

[**Note:** You can speak in favour of both hard work and smart work. You cannot completely oppose either of them, though you should make your points in a firm manner.]

18. Are Strikes Justifiable?

In favour of strikes:

1. Strikes are one of the few tools available to the employees and workers against the exploitation done by the powerful ones occupying higher positions. Without the option of strikes being available to them, their exploitation will go on. Strike is one of the methods to demand and get your rights.

2. Strikes have been used since time immemorial to protect the rights of the powerless ones. Even our freedom fighters used methods like nationwide strikes against the foreign rule.

3. Strikes create awareness among the workers and employees about their own rights. Many of them don't know their own rights.

4. Strikes help maintain balance of power between the management and the labour.

Against strikes:

1. Strikes disrupt life of a common man. When there's a strike of the doctors, the patients die, as they don't get proper treatment. Whenever there's a strike of the railways, buses, taxis, etc., the common man cannot reach his destination. The ultimate sufferer of any strike is the innocent common man.

2. Strikes have become a method of getting legitimate and illegitimate demands fulfilled. People just go on a strike and think they can get whatever they want. Many strikes are done for no proper reason but for personal gains. In other words, strikes are being misused.

3. In some fields (such as health, security, essential services), strikes are absolutely unjustifiable.

4. Strikes worsen the financial health of a company, and may even cause a company to go out of business. This may render both striking and other workers jobless and can even ruin their careers.

5. Strikes affect the tourists as well. When they can't get the services they expect in a nation, they carry a negative image of that nation in their minds. This way strikes ruin the image of a nation.

6. Strikes repel the investors who could otherwise make permanent investments in a country. This way strikes act against the economic progress of a country.

Our suggestion: Strikes must always be used only as the last resort, and not the first one. Strikes must not be used to get all kinds of demands fulfilled, but should only be used against exploitation. Moreover, when a strike can result in the deaths of people, it cannot be justified at all. Strike is not a weapon to misuse.

19. Time is Money

In favour:

1. Time and money are closely related. The more time a person invests in making money, the richer he may get. Therefore, we can say that time is money. Both are strongly correlated.

2. When a person invests in a real estate or shares, his investment may grow with time. A good example is Mr. Warren Buffet, one of the richest men, whose investments multiplied with time. So, we can say that time is money.

3. Why do we spend so much time in offices? Because we get money for that! Time is money.

4. A person may get the best treatments for his health condition if he has money, and this way he can add some more time to his life (though some people will differ on this point). Therefore, money can give us some more time.

5. A rich person doesn't have to worry about how he will earn his bread and butter; instead he may do what he likes. This freedom may not be available to a poor person. This way, money can buy a person some time to enjoy!

Against:

1. Life is nothing but a collection of seconds, hours and days. In other words, life itself is a measure of time a person has! How can, then, time not be more important than money? And if it is, how can we say that time is money?

2. A terminally ill person can offer all his wealth, but may not be able to buy another second to live! Finally, he may die, leaving all his wealth to others. Time is more important than wealth. Napoleon Bonaparte once said to someone, "You can ask me for anything you like, except time."

3. People who spend all their time running behind money may not get time to live and time to spend with their loved ones. Therefore, chase of money may, in fact, reduce the time a person has!

4. Some people are so greedy that they can trade a long life for a short but rich life. To them, money is more important than time!

Our suggestion: This topic assesses your thinking abilities. Time is something more than money, and time is something that people need to make money. Both time and money are important, and both are two different identities. Investing time in money-making activities can help a person live a better life; still time is not all about making money. Since you wouldn't like to sound too greedy, take a stand that shows that you care not only about money but about life as a whole. Provide suitable examples to support your view.

20. Red

1. Red colour signifies danger. We do not jump a red signal and we do not immediately touch an object marked red, as it may be a 'danger sign'. A red alert is a warning of the coming danger. Even some of the poisonous snakes have red skin-colour.

2. Red colour easily draws attention of people. It evokes strong emotions. This fact has been taken into account by various business organizations while designing their logos. That's why there are so many logos which use red colour. It is also said that red colour enhances the appetite of a person; that's why it is a favourite colour of the restaurants. Red colour may also indicate the energy and enthusiasm an organisation puts in its business. *(**Note:** If you are appearing in a GD for an MBA seat, you may want to discuss this point first.)*

3. In politics, red may refer to communism. Red colour, the colour of blood, is associated with revolutions, many of which were accompanied by sacrifices of thousands of labours. Therefore,

in communism, red colour is quite significant. It can be seen in the flags of the communist countries (China, USSR (presently Russia), etc.).

4. Red colour is also associated with love. The colour of a rose is red, and it is said that red colour fastens the heart-beat of a person. Also, red colour signifies warmth. Red-carpet welcome is given to the special guests. A Red Letter Day is a special day.

5. In the war, red is the colour of sacrifice and courage, again because it's the colour of blood and the brave soldiers shed blood while fighting the enemy. Mars, the red planet, got its name from Mars, the Roman God of war.

6. Red is the colour of bridal dresses in India. Red-tape refers to bureaucracy. Ruby, a precious gemstone, is red in colour.

7. A person, who has been caught red-handed, has just committed a crime.

8. Red colour has the largest wavelength among the visible colours; beyond red begins the infrared range, which is used in the night vision equipment, wireless communication, etc. (*Note:* Don't use just plain facts; site some uses of them. Plain facts are hard to discuss.)

9. Red may be the colour of your favourite sports team's uniform. You may discuss the latest accomplishments of that team.

Our suggestion: While given a colour to discuss, never jump to say it is a colour. This mistake is quite common. Instead, you may begin with what it reminds you of or what is significant about it. Avoid discussing less important points, or discuss them when nothing else remains to be discussed (For example, a team's uniform colour). Also, take care to mention only positive points while associating any colour with any religion or ideology. You should not hurt anyone's religious feelings.

21. Blue

1. Blue is one of the most favourite colours of the corporate world. The bluechip companies are some of the most reputed ones; stock market indices (Sensex, Nifty, America's Dow Jones, etc.) often follow the indices of the bluechip firms. Blue is associated with reliability and loyalty. Banks and Airlines use it in their logos. Many security personnel too wear blue uniforms. You might have noticed that many of the social networking sites (Facebook, Twitter, LinkedIn, etc.) use blue colour in branding, because blue colour is also one of the most favourite colours of the entire world population.

2. Blue is the colour of the vast sky (that's why the expression, 'it came to me out of the blue', i.e., it came unexpectedly and suddenly). Blue is also the colour of the deep ocean. Many cheerful songs and poems have been written about it. Even the ice at the poles and the icebergs in the ocean appear blue sometimes. Sapphire gemstone is also blue in colour.

3. Blue ink is used in writing because it is understood that blue colour has a calming effect on mind. Blue colour is often associated with calmness and cool (while, as we discussed, red is associated with hot/warm). It may have some connection with the fact that the blue colour has one of the shortest wavelengths (while the red colour has the largest wavelength).

4. Blue is also a favourite colour of the dress makers and designers. Who can forget blue jeans?

5. Blue colour has been used in the flags of many countries; sometimes alone, sometimes in conjugation with other colours. (Examples: Argentina, Greece, the USA, etc.) The Indian tricolour has a blue-coloured Ashok chakra in the centre.

6. Blue colour is sometimes associated with sadness and depression. Depression is often called 'blue' or 'blue feeling'.

7. Blue has been the colour of the Indian cricket team's uniform for a long time.

Our suggestion: You can also discuss what significance the blue colour has in your life, but it must not be boring and certainly not too lengthy; and others should find it interesting and should be able to discuss it.

22. Green

1. Green, the colour of plants, is often associated with environment. Green is environment-friendly. Without plants, there can be no life. Greenery is not only important but it also looks good to human eyes. Green energy is the energy produced using environment-friendly, non-polluting methods and resources. Green economy is the economy that also cares about the environment. Green movement is also associated with nature and environment (you might have heard or read about 'GO GREEN'). Ocean and lake water may appear green because of phytoplankton, algae, or plants inside the water.

2. It is a corporate social responsibility **(CSR)** of the business organizations to support the welfare of the environment and take 'green' initiatives. A company which harms the environment may lose people's goodwill. Many companies 'go green' by taking steps to reduce pollution, and this brings a lot of free and positive publicity to them.

3. Green may remind you of 'the green revolution' of India, which helped the nation fulfil its demand of foodgrains. Use of fertilizers, providing financial credit to farmers, improvement of irrigation facilities and use of high-quality seeds helped the nation become self-sufficient in foodgrains.

4. In many cultures, green colour is associated with abundance, prosperity, fertility and life; perhaps because of its association with plants and grass (grass spreads fast). Green colour is used

by the healthcare product companies, especially for Ayurvedic products. The Indian tricolour also has green in it.

5. Green colour is a part of many flags. Most of the Islamic nations have green colour in their flags. Many nations use green colour in their flags to represent their rich greenery.

6. Green is the colour of banknotes of some countries (including the USA). The precious Emerald stone is also green in colour.

7. Green traffic signal means it's safe to move ahead.

Our suggestion: When you are given the topic 'Green', talk liberally about the environment and why it is important for the businesses to 'go green' and support the green movement.

23. Black

1. In business, black symbolizes power, authority and exclusivity. You might have noticed that people in high positions love to dress in black. Judges and lawyers also wear black. Black colour in expensive cars (BMW, Mercedes, etc.) is people's favourite. Black colour is acceptable on most of the formal occasions.

2. Black is the colour of dark. People associate black with horror and mystery; and it's quite natural because the human eyes cannot see in the dark. In movies, horror and crime scenes are often shot in the dark. Children fear dark, while the teenagers like black (that's why black colour is liberally used in products made for teens; be it jackets, T-shirts, jeans, shoes, bikes, even video games). Black is the colour we see in the universe, much of which is yet to be explored.

3. People use black flags to protest against someone, to show that that person is not welcome there.

4. In many Western countries, people wear black while going for a funeral.

5. Black is also associated with bad and evil. Black magic, black mail, black marketing of goods, they all are associated with either bad or evil.

6. Black colour absorbs sunlight and its heat; it is used in the solar water heaters and solar cookers, and pipes carrying hot water. This may also be a reason why people prefer to wear black in winters.

7. 'Black' is the name of a Bollywood movie which highlights the life of a blind person. You may discuss how painful it is to lose eyesight, and why and how should the society take care of blind people. (But don't forget that not everyone understands Hindi or watch Hindi movies.)

8. Black may remind you of the black-board, or your karate black belt, or your lawyer's coat, or other black things.

Our suggestion: It may be better to discuss the positive points about 'black' first, or to discuss the negative ones in a positive manner. It will give an impression that you think positive, but try to make it interesting.

24. White

1. White, no doubt, stands for peace and calm. White flag in war means offer of peace and surrender. Many NGOs, including Red Cross, use white colour in their flags and logos. White pigeons symbolize peace. The Indian tricolour also has white colour in it.

2. White also stands for purity and cleanliness. That's why restaurants use white plates, so that the original colour of the food items in them is visible clearly; plus it shows that the plates are clean. White is also used in mixers, electric cookers, sinks and bathroom tiles. Even hospitals use white colour on walls. Hotels (and the Indian railways) use white bed-sheets and pillow covers.

3. White colour also stands for truth and good. You might have noted that good fairies in the cartoon serials and children's books are dressed in white. (Coincidentally, Mahatma Gandhi, the man who is considered to be the messenger of truth and peace, dressed in white!) 'Whitewash' and 'White lie' mean something untrue being presented as truth.

4. White may remind you of 'the White Revolution' of India, which made our country one of the largest producers of milk and helped us meet our population's requirements.

5. White is a favourite colour for the bridal dresses in the West.

6. In spirituality, there is a special place for white. Many spiritual gurus dress in white. Almost in every religion, white is associated with a God or a hero.

7. Snow is white in colour, so white may also be a sign of cold weather. When there's a snowfall, everything gets covered in white.

8. White may also be the colour of a sports team. It is also the colour of the Indian Navy's dress, and cricket teams wear white in test matches. Moreover, it is a colour of many schools' uniforms. (Probably, many participants in the GD you participate in will be wearing white shirts! It's a formal colour for dresses.)

9. White colour reflects sunlight; that's why people prefer white clothes in summers.

25. Black and White

1. Black and white are two contrasting colours. To some people, it may remind of the contrasting qualities and skills required in the members of a business team, so that they can supplement each other whenever needed. For instance, the extrovert members may take care of the media relations, while the introvert ones may take care of the operations and finance part. Some

members may have the marketing skills while others may have human resource management skills. Many top business leaders feel that if the members of a team have contrasting qualities, it can be good for the health of the organisation.

2. To most of the elderly people, black and white may remind of the television programs and movies of the times when they were young, when colour TV was a luxury available only to the rich ones. You may think that it is a thing of the past, but it is not so! Now, when almost all the programs, movies and TV commercials are coloured, black and white presents a nice alternative because it easily draws attention of the people in this coloured world. You might have seen the recent black and white ads on TV. Some latest movies have been made in black and white (including the academy award winner 'The Artist' (2011 movie)). It seems like good old days are back again!

3. You may discuss how much the country (or the world) has changed from the times when black and white movies were made, and whether this change was entirely good or there were some negative impacts too.

4. The Buddhist symbol of Yin and Yang is often coloured in black and white. It symbolizes that contrasts co-exist in the world. For instance, dark exists with light, good with bad, happiness with sadness, etc.

5. Black and white photos of the freedom fighters of India are there over the internet.

Our suggestion: Black and white reminds us of the contrasting qualities that coexist in the nature, or in businesses, or among people, or even in one person. It also reminds of the fact that a person must be prepared to face the good and the bad times in life; that he should be able to appreciate joy and tolerate sorrow; that life is not always the same; that change is inevitable. Good and bad times come even in businesses (growth periods and recessions).

26. Red vs. Blue

1. In the world of business, red vs. blue is often interpreted as cola war between the two cola giants – Coke and Pepsi; Coke being represented by red and Pepsi by blue (After reading about red colour and blue colour, you might have understood why the cola companies use red and blue colours). The competition between Coke and Pepsi to capture the markets of the world has been there since a century. While Coke sells more cola than Pepsi in many countries, Pepsi has a strong foothold in the Indian market. Coke has tried very hard to win the Indian market from Pepsi, but the war is expected to last long. Both the companies spend billions of dollars on their marketing campaigns. (You may discuss the marketing campaigns in detail.)

2. Red vs. blue may refer to a competition between two political parties, two sports teams, even two countries (red usually represents communist countries or ideology). Sometimes, the USSR is shown with red and the USA is shown with blue. You may be reminded of the cold war era when the two superpowers were close to a third world war. China may also be represented by red; hence, red vs. blue may refer to the competition between China and the USA to become the number one economy of the world.

3. Red and blue, like white and black, are contrasting colours. While red stands for warmth, blue stands for cool (as discussed earlier). Red vs. blue may remind you of a conflict between two contrasting qualities or people with contrasting qualities. (Read the topic 'Black and White' for details.) Red and blue inks are used for writing and checking respectively. It may remind you of your school days (how you struggled to keep red marks and big zeros away from your homework!)

4. Red vs. Blue may remind you of remarkable cricket matches between Zimbabwe/West Indies and India/England. There

had been a match in which Kapil Dev had scored 175 against Zimbabwe, without which India couldn't have won the 1983 world cup (though the dresses of the players might have been different then).

Our suggestion: Since the topic is 'red vs. blue' and not 'red and blue', try to stick with the points that show a duel, a competition between the two colours and what they represent.

27. Gold

1. Gold is a precious metal and is used for monetary exchanges between the nations. In 1991, the Indian economy was in turmoil and we had to mortgage a part of our gold reserves for the foreign exchange. Since then, we have never faced such tough times. This incidence is very important in India's corporate history because only after this, India adopted the policy of liberalisation and disinvestment, according to which, a government allows privatization of at least some public sector companies.

2. Gold is used for making jewellery, and we live in a society in which jewellery has a very special place. India is the largest consumer of gold; mainly because the Indians wear a lot of jewellery. Gold jewellery and coins are bought on various occasions (including *'dhanteras'*).

3. Gold also refers to the Olympic gold medals. Till 2008, India had won only one individual Olympic gold medal (won by shooter Abhinav Bindra). You can discuss what we need to do to win more gold medals in the Olympic games and make our nation proud (provide our athletes better facilities for training, give them more respect, arrange for better coaching, etc.).

4. Gold may remind people of 'Old is Gold', i.e., old things and times are better than new ones. (Don't over-discuss it because it is altogether a separate topic.)

5. Gold is getting very expensive day-by-day. Prices are rising steeply. In 2000, a person used to pay Rs. 4,400 for 10 grams of gold, while in 2011, he had to pay Rs. 26,400 for the same quantity.

6. Gold may also refer to golden colour (metallic gold). 50th anniversary of an event is called golden jubilee. You may also discuss golden age of the Indian economy. Golden trophies are given for the highest achievement in a field, so gold is everybody's dream.

7. Since gold is the metal which doesn't react easily, gold is a symbol of purity as well. You might have heard 'his heart is as pure as gold'.

Our suggestion: If you are appearing for a GD for an MBA finance seat, it may be quite beneficial to talk about economic interpretations of the word 'gold', but add a point or two from general interpretations too. It will show you are not just a bookworm.

28. Old is Gold

In favour:

1. In old times, there was no cut-throat competition as is today. There were ample seats for worthy aspirants in the colleges. There were enough jobs for educated people, and graduation degrees did matter much more. People were content with less and everyone was not running behind money. People were not as greedy as they are today, and they did not invent new methods to deceive others and get hands on their money. At least the vegetables were grown naturally, and the cows were not given hormonal injections to get more milk from them.

2. In old times, there was peace of mind. Since competition was less, people didn't overstretch themselves to perform better and better. Also, they used to have ample time to meet their friends and relatives. They used to write letters instead of sending quick

SMSs and they used to see each other in person instead of using social networking sites and sharing photos.

3. In old times, there used to be joint families, in which workload was shared among the members, and so were expenses. Ill and old members, kids and financially weak members were taken care of properly. There were fewer mental disorders and lifestyle diseases, as tension was not the integral part of people's lives (as it is now).

4. India's golden days were in its glorious past. Some experts say that India was the largest economy of the world a few centuries ago. This is also why we can say old is gold.

5. Many people believe that old movies were better than the new ones, because they were more sensible. So is said about songs and music too.

6. Since consumerism was less prevalent, people were not judged by their expensive clothes and possessions but by their behaviour and character. People earned less but they enjoyed more.

7. Old antiques have high monetary value, so sometimes it is said that an old thing is as precious as gold. So is true about an old wine. ***(Caution:*** *Don't use this point unless you want to add some humour to a too serious discussion. This point is bound to be taken lightly)*.

Against:

1. In old days, there were fewer treatments available for diseases, therefore, more number of people died from them. Infant mortality rates were quite high when compared to present rates.

2. Since there was no (or little) competition, an individual's full potential could not be realised. People used to take their works lightly and they didn't give their best every time.

3. In joint families of old times, and individual used to get less freedom to live as he wanted. He had to be the part of an

already established system. The rate of nation's (and individual's) progress was also slow in old days.

4. Of course, there were fewer facilities and luxuries available to people. Luxury not only makes life more comfortable, but it motivates a person to perform better in life. People dream of buying a BMW or a manor one day, and they work hard for it.

5. Time keeps changing. What we have today will get old tomorrow. Therefore, by the rule of 'old is gold', it will also be gold some day!

Our suggestion: Most people tend to agree that old is gold, therefore, you should not entirely reject the statement 'Old is Gold'. You should accept it, at least to an extent.

29. Is the Ban on Plastic Bags in Cities Justified?

In favour of plastic bags:

1. Plastic bags are cheaper than cloth bags. Even poor people can afford them, as they are provided free with goods.

2. Plastic bags are reusable, while paper bags can't be used as many times.

3. Plastic bags can protect the goods against rain and water spills.

4. Trees are cut for the raw-material required to manufacture paper bags, therefore, using plastic bags is a good alternative.

Against plastic bags:

1. Worse effects of plastic on the environment are well-known. Plastic takes a long time to degrade and degenerate, and it haunts the environment for a long time. Its bad impacts on the environment outweigh its benefits.

2. Very few plastic bags are recycled every year. Most of the time, they are thrown away in the environment to pollute it. These throw-away bags may suffocate children and animals if accidentally ingested.

3. Plastic bags block drain pipes when they are thrown away with the wet garbage. And people don't think twice before throwing them because these bags are so cheap.

4. The fertility of the soil gets worse when plastic becomes a part of it.

5. Plastic bags, which are not properly disposed off, create an ugly scene in the city; and they remain visible for very long time.

Our suggestion: Plastic bags must only be used when there is no alternative. It is justified to ban plastic bags in some cities where they cause too much environmental problem.

30. Internet: A Boon or A Bane?

In favour of internet:

1. Internet has made this vast world a global village. Now, we can't just talk to a person in any part of the world but we can see him while doing so! We can share documents, information, pictures and videos with anyone in the world within no time. Internet has helped human beings unite.

2. Internet has reduced the need of paperwork, which means we do not need to cut trees to get paper to write anymore. We can simply type and send a report or a document to anyone. We can read e-books.

3. Internet is the fastest way to send news and information in any part of the world.

4. Internet helps millions of students learn the subject they want, in detail and without a teacher's help. It wouldn't have been possible just by books. Students even get degrees by taking online classes and exams.

5. Perhaps there is no information which is not available on the internet. If you want to know something, all you need to do is type it into a search engine, and search!

6. A person ternet.

7. Since all the content over the internet cannot be scrutinized, children using internet are exposed to a lot of inappropriate information in the form of edited or unedited pictures, videos, writings, etc., which may not be suitable for them.

8. Internet is certainly not the safest way to use banking services. Online frauds are quite common. Moreover, we do not have sufficiently strict internet laws in India to prevent such frauds.

9. Internet has also created a distance between the people who earlier used to meet personally instead of writing online messages.

Our suggestion: Like all other technologies, internet can be used or misused. Ultimately, it depends on us what we do with it. Internet, if used for creative purposes, is certainly a boon to the society. You should speak in favour of internet because most organisations use internet these days; though you may add a word of caution too.

31. Control Over Social Networking Websites – Justified?

In favour:

1. A lot of inappropriate content is published on the social networking sites everyday. It can be in the form of blasphemous content, sexual content, foul language or derogatory content about the well-known people. This might create the atmosphere conducive to riots and violence. Therefore, it may be necessary to have some amount of control over the content published on social networking sites.

2. Since children also use social networking sites, it is important to ensure that they do not learn inappropriate things from these sites. Thus, some amount of control is justified.

3. Anything, when kept fully out of control, may be misused by anti-social elements (terrorists, smugglers, etc.). Moreover, it is

alleged sometimes that the owners of the social networking sites misuse them to promote a specific culture.

Against:

1. Social networking sites are, perhaps, the only place where people get freedom to express themselves fully. They say what they want and they post what they want. They express their joys, sorrows, anger against bad policies; they post their problems and seek solutions; they unite when needed (such as in Jessica Lall case, when people organised candle march in Delhi, using social networking sites to invite people). Why take away their freedom of expression?

2. Sometimes, the governments of some nations do not want people to come together and unite against the misrule of the government. As a result, whenever a fear of people's uprising appears, the first thing they try to do is impose a ban on social networking websites. (It happened in Egypt, Syria, Libya and many other countries. Even China has banned the social networking sites intermittently.) If a permanent control is implemented on these sites, it will be more like ending people's only hope of uniting in such countries. Social networking sites must be kept free in every nation.

3. There is already a moderation policy of these websites. People accept the terms and conditions of these sites before they start using them, and when they violate the rules, they can be banned from these sites. Any inappropriate content, when reported, is removed from the sites. Why impose more control?

Our suggestion: While complete control over social networking websites cannot be justified, a little moderation is okay and, perhaps, important too.

32. Freedom of Press – Why is It Important?

1. Free media or press is known as the fourth pillar of a democracy because it acts freely and lets people know about good and

bad policies and actions of their government, and in this way, affects the opinion of the people. Therefore, we can say that press plays an important role in a democracy by helping people judge their representatives. When press is not free, it cannot put an unbiased image of a leader before people. For transparency and impartiality, it is important that the press is kept completely free from all sorts of controls (except in the times of a national emergency such as a war, when secrecy needs to be maintained).

2. If the press is not free, it can be misused by those who have control over it. People might be served distorted facts and wrong data, and they may be kept in the dark. Mismanagement and corruption will prevail. Therefore, it is important that the press is kept free from anybody's control.

3. It has been noted that in those countries where press is not free, fundamental human rights are not respected. People in such countries are not free to live as they like. Therefore, an individual's personal freedom depends a lot on the freedom of press in his nation.

4. When the press is free, the reporters can write the truth, because they know they will not be punished even if that truth goes against the rich and the powerful people of the country. India's press has helped police put many powerful criminals behind the bars. If press cannot publish the truth, it is almost useless.

5. A free press indicates that a nation is truly free. It attracts investors, tourists and businesses towards that nation. Who would like to visit or invest in a country where even press is not free? Free press might ensure justice.

6. Freedom of press is also important because press plays a very important role in creating awareness among the people. It makes people aware of where the country is lagging behind, what steps should be taken to ensure progress and whether those steps are being or not being taken. Therefore, free press is a necessity of any nation, which wants to prosper and develop.

33. Rapidly Growing Population of India – A Boon or Bane?

Boon:

1. More than half of India's population is below the age of 25. This means that we will have a very large working class in a few years, and this population will definitely play its part in the development of our nation. It will also earn huge sums for the country.

2. Moreover, it will provide a vast pool of manpower for the country. This is quite favourable for our nation because it attracts the service sector multinational companies which want to get their services done at much lower cost in India (Many software companies, animation companies and BPO companies come into this category).

3. More minds mean more talent, and more people mean more earning hands. India has a huge talented population. If used effectively, it can be a great advantage to our country.

4. Cheap labour means an advantage in the fields of construction, mining, manufacturing, etc.

Bane:

1. Huge population also means more mouths to feed. We have not been able to provide enough food to our current population. How can we possibly arrange sufficient food for a lot more population? To make the matter worse, India is expected to become the most populous country of the world by 2025, surpassing China.

2. People who are young today will get old one day. Who will be able to take care of such a huge population then? Or shall we keep increasing our population forever?

3. Unemployment has always been a problem in India. The reason – we cannot create sufficient jobs for ever-growing population.

4. Population causes problems in every walk of life. There are no sufficient seats in schools, no sufficient beds in hospitals, no sufficient electricity or water to meet our huge population's demands, no seats in trains or buses, and huge traffic jams on roads. How long can our infrastructure stand such a huge pressure? Our resources are getting scarce everyday.

5. Standard of living has also suffered a lot because of huge population of India. Government too cannot arrange sufficient amounts of money needed to be spent on the personal development of so many people.

Our suggestion: While there may be some advantages of having a huge population, it has proved to be a bane to our nation so far. We must take the necessary steps to control the growth of our population before the situation gets out of control.

34. India-Pakistan Relations

1. **In general:** Political relations between India and Pakistan have always been tense. Pakistan separated from India in 1947, and since then both the countries have fought three full-scale wars (in 1947, in 1965 and in 1971), after the sadistic riots that took place at the time of division (more than a million people had lost their lives in those riots). Two of these wars were fought over Kashmir, while the third one because West Pakistan's (now Pakistan) attack on East Pakistan (now Bangladesh) was causing a heavy migration of the Bangladeshi people to India. Besides these wars, there had been a small scale war in the Kargil sector of Jammu and Kashmir in 1999. Terrorism that originates from the soil of Pakistan has also been a cause of tension between the two nations. Actions of ISI, the intelligence agency of Pakistan, have always been the bone of contention between the two countries. It is understood that ISI sponsors terrorism against India; while Pakistan alleges Indian intelligence agency RAW of doing the same in Pakistan. The relations seemed to

be coming back on track on various occasions, such as when the 'Samjhauta Express' train was started between the two countries, when the Indian prime ministers travelled to Pakistan and the Pakistani PMs and Presidents visited India, but it could not make much difference. Pakistan does not recognise Kashmir as a part of India. The latest factors that deteriorated the bilateral relations were attacks on the Indian parliament (in 2001) and on Mumbai city (in 2008). Pakistan doesn't support India's claim for a permanent seat in the United Nations Security Council (UNSC) either. Though the people of both the nations have not abandoned hopes of better relations, it might take a long time before the relations get better and the peace prevails.

2. **Cultural relations:** Both the countries share a very similar set of cultural traits and traditions. Not only the dresses and food habits of people of both the countries are quite similar but so are the problems and challenges the people of the two countries are facing. Both the countries have large number of people who live below poverty line. Illiteracy and unemployment are major problems in both the countries. Every year, many Pakistanis come to visit the religious places in India and many Indians go to Pakistan for the same reason. Bollywood movies are very popular in Pakistan and the Pakistani singers, actors and artists work, perform and live in India. People of both the countries love cricket. Hindi is very similar to Urdu.

3. **Economic relations:** Since India and Pakistan are neighbours, it is quite natural for them to have economic relations. But it would be correct to say that the impact of political relations between the two countries can be clearly seen on the economic relations too. Total trade (import + export) between the two countries has reached about 2.6 billion USD (till 2011-12), while it could have been much more if an environment of mutual trust had been there. India exports dyes and chemicals, petroleum products, fabrics, spices, drugs, plastic products, etc. to Pakistan,

while Pakistan exports cement, leather, nuts, petroleum products, metals, organic chemicals, etc. to India. There's a great scope for better trade relations between the two nations.

35. India-China Relations

Political and cultural relations: India and China are the two most populated nations and two of the oldest civilisations of the world. Both the countries had traded through silk route in the past, and Buddhism, which originated in India, became a major religion in China. In between 600-700AD, the Chinese monk, Huen-Tsang came to India and remained here for seventeen years. Both the countries have been ruled by foreign powers in the past, and Mahatma Gandhi had supported the Chinese people's struggle for independence. In 1954, both the countries signed the 'Panchsheel Agreement', whose five principles were 'mutual respect for each other's territory and sovereignty, equality, non-aggression, non-interference in each-other's affairs, and peaceful co-existence'. Yet India and China fought a war in 1962 (Sino-Indian war). Since then, both the countries have never regained complete mutual trust. Moreover, China has always been a supporter of Pakistan and this has only worsened the relations. It is alleged that China supplies missile technology and nuclear technology to Pakistan. In a recent event, China told the Indian oil-exploration companies to keep off from the South China Sea, where the Indian companies have joint ventures with the Vietnamese companies. It is said that India made Agni-V missile with a range of 5,000+ kilometres keeping China in mind.

Economic relations: China and India are the two fastest growing major economies of the world. Both have risen from a state of extreme poverty (in fact, poverty is still prevalent in both the societies) to become major trading partners. In 2011, the bilateral trade between the two nations reached 74 billion USD, but the trade deficit data is highly in China's favour. India imports much more from China than what it exports to China. India exports iron ores, copper, precious stones, plastic, fabric, salt, machinery, etc. to China, while China exports machinery, fertilisers, nuclear reactors related products, boilers, etc. to India.

(Read the next topic **'India vs. China'**)

36. India vs. China

1. **General comparison:** Area-wise China is far bigger than India, but by population, India is not far behind. It is estimated that India will surpass China in population by 2025, though it also means that India will have more young working population. While India is a democracy, China is ruled by a single party led by the communist leaders (Not having a democratic form of government is, as some experts believe, the biggest weakness of China). China's armed forces are bigger than the Indian armed forces and China has longer range missiles too. But India believes that it has sufficient power to meet China's challenge. Literacy rates in China are higher and experts say that China has a better healthcare system, perhaps because China spends much more on healthcare and education than India does. In infrastructure, no doubt, China is far ahead, as it spends a larger part of its GDP on infrastructure than India does. In Olympic games, China has won more gold medals than India did (till 2008). Life expectancy is also better in China. On the other hand, India has a large English speaking population while China lacks this advantage. That's why India has stronger BPO sector. India is ahead in IT sector too. Many experts also believe that the Chinese government artificially undervalues its currency Yuan. Many believe that China has a worse record in the field of fundamental human rights. Since China isn't a democracy, decision making is somewhat faster in China because the ruling party has all the rights in its hands.

2. **Economic comparison:** India and China are the two fastest growing major economies of the world. While China has a

strong manufacturing sector, India has strong knowledge-based industries. As for now, China seems to be ahead of India. India's Gross Domestic Product (Purchasing Power Parity) was around 4.4 trillion USD in 2011, while China's GDP was 11.2 trillion USD in 2011. In the same year, India's GDP grew at 7.8% growth rate, while the growth rate of China's GDP was 9.5%. In 2011, India's international trade was approx. 800 billion USD while China's international trade was approx. 3,500 billion USD. India also has some advantages over China. The Indian economy is understood to be more insulated to a global economic crisis than China's economy, because India's GDP is not as much dependent on exports as China's GDP is. India is ahead of China in IT industry and it has more number of English-speaking people. Some experts believe that India might be able to overtake China in the long run. Now let's talk about how China managed to develop so fast.

Secrets behind China's economic miracle: We can say that China took some right decisions at the right time:

1. China set up the Special Economic Zones near its coasts to boost its exports.
2. The Chinese government, being the one-party government, can freely take all the decisions rapidly. They utilized this advantage and gave a large part of agricultural land to the investors to set up industries.
3. The Chinese government announced tax concessions for those investors, who set up companies in the developmentally backward areas and rural sectors.
4. China has the availability of cheap labour.
5. China opened its markets to foreign investors much before India did. Its economic reforms began in 1978.

6. China spent more on infrastructure, research and development and providing skill training to its workers.

Our suggestion: It can be concluded that India will have to work hard to compete with China, as the latter seems to be doing quite well. However, nothing is impossible, and India can win the race if it tries hard.

37. BRIC/BRICS

'BRIC' refers to **B**razil, **R**ussia, **I**ndia and **C**hina. These are some of the fast growing major economies of the world. (South Africa joined the group in 2011 and the acronym became BRICS.) It is expected that these countries are going to do economically quite well in the coming times. China and India, the fastest growing major economies of the world, are expected to do better than the rest two. The BRICS countries account for almost half of the world's population. When the economic crisis of 2008 hit the world, the world looked at the BRICS countries to play a bigger role to get the world out of the crisis.

In the BRICS Summit of 2011, the leaders of five countries met in China and they called for better economic relations and coordination among themselves. They urged UN to take harder steps against terrorism and terror sponsors. They also decided to use their own currencies for mutual trade. They also called for a larger role of BRICS in the United Nations Security Council.

(If you have a basic understanding of the groups of countries, such as BRICS, SAARC, OPEC, etc., it could be quite helpful in a group discussion or an interview. No need to get into smaller details unless you aspire for a post-MBA education.)

38. OPEC

OPEC stands for the **O**rganisation of the **P**etroleum **E**xporting **C**ountries. This organisation of twelve oil-producing countries is important because it has certain control over the oil prices in the world market, as it determines how much oil has to be produced and exported. As mentioned earlier, there are twelve OPEC countries in total (some of them being Saudi Arabia, the UAE, Iran, Iraq, Kuwait, Qatar and Nigeria). OPEC has its headquarters in Vienna. The objective behind the creation of this organisation was to safeguard the interests of the oil producing nations and to stop unnecessary fluctuations in the oil prices in the world market. However, these countries have been alleged of increasing the oil prices artificially by decreasing the production of oil, in order to increase their revenues.

39. SAARC

SAARC stands for **S**outh **A**sian **A**ssociation for **R**egional **C**ooperation. It is a group of the South Asian nations – India, Pakistan, Bangladesh, Sri Lanka, Nepal, Maldives, Bhutan and Afghanistan (Afghanistan joined SAARC in 2007). The main objective behind the creation of SAARC was to promote the welfare of the people of the South Asian region, to promote cultures of the member nations, and to boost trade and economic growth. (Another, and unstated, objective was to demand more benefits in trade from the developed nations so that the poor people of South Asia could benefit.) However, some comparatively smaller member countries keep complaining that the SAARC summits are often dominated by the issues pertaining to larger members (India and Pakistan). For instance, in one of the SAARC summits, India raised the issue of terrorism, and it is alleged that this issue eclipsed the issues of smaller states.

The SAARC members have signed a free trade agreement called SAFTA (South Asian Free Trade Area) in order to promote free trade between the member countries. Though all the tariff barriers have not been removed yet, many have been reduced substantially and some have been removed entirely. Free trade agreements play an important role in boosting trade in a region.

40. Unity in Diversity – A Gift or A Curse?

A gift:

1. Unity in diversity in our country shows that people of India are broad-minded and tolerant, that they can live with each other, no matter how diverse their religious beliefs, customs, traditions, languages, or ways of living may be.

2. Unity in diversity is good for a nation's economy because it works in the favour of tourism. When people visit a different nation, what they want to see is different ways of living. In India, this diversity is so huge that a tourist may not explore the nation completely even after years of roaming. If used wisely, this diversity can make India a favourite tourist destination of the world.

3. When the people of various cultures come together to live with each other, along come their diverse cultures and traditions; and each culture has its own strength. Some cultures emphasize on modern, scientific ways of living, others on ancient wisdom, still others on peace and prosperity, etc. These cultures learn from each other and adopt each other's values. This makes a society strong. India, a country which has people who speak different languages, follow different religions and celebrate so many different festivals every year, is very rich in diversity. When these cultures unite, they form a great civilisation. Perhaps India is the only nation where Hindus, Muslims, Christians, Sikhs, Buddhists and people belonging to other religions celebrate each other's festivals. A Hindu decorates his house on Christmas; Muslims celebrate Diwali; Sikhs visit Churches and Christians celebrate Holi, Eid and Gurpurab. All this in one nation is extraordinary.

4. When people experience so much diversity in their own country, they can mentally adjust in any society of the world. They can live in any part of the world, no matter how diverse it is. The

Indian people have been able to adjust in almost every society of the world. Indians are there in every nation, and they are living well.

5. Diversity teaches a nation how to face various kinds of challenges. For instance, since India has high mountains, deep seas, hot deserts and dense forests, it also has the soldiers who can fight in any terrain. UN has sent the Indian soldiers on various peace-keeping missions in different nations, and they have proved their mettle in those nations.

Against:

1. When the people of different religions, regions and cultures fight with each other in the name of religion, language or region, their attitudes become a threat to the nation's integrity. Riots and mass murders take place; people begin to hate each other; they do not cooperate with each other. Interests of the nation become second priority, and their differences occupy their minds. This may only happen when there's diversity. In India, there have been many communal riots in the past years.

2. Diversity provides room for divisive politics. Some shrewd politicians divide people in the name of religion, caste, language, etc. only to get vote of particular segments of people.

3. When there's religious diversity, the nation needs to create various different places of worship for the people of different communities and religions. As a result, India has more places of worship than colleges, hospitals, bus stands, etc.

Our suggestion: When people learn to live with each other and respect each other's culture, diversity can become one of the greatest treasures available to a country. It does not only look good, but also adds to the development of the nation. India is fortunate to have so much diversity. The need of the hour is to learn to use it wisely. People should learn to live in peace and harmony.

41. Reservation for Women in Politics

In favour:

1. It is a matter of shame that when we talk about women's participation in politics, India ranks after the top 100 nations, behind our neighbours, Pakistan, Nepal and Bangladesh. And this is despite the fact that the Indian women have proved themselves in the top positions (such as Prime Minister) of India. Only around 10% or so members of our parliament are women. Why not give women a fair chance by reserving some seats for them?

2. Gone are the days when the role of women was restricted to home. Now they are competing with men in almost every field. Women are serving in the army, healthcare, law, research, in every field. Why not in politics then?

3. Women, in many fields, have proved to be as good managers as men are, or even better than men in some cases. Why not give them a chance to manage the nation?

4. Women have been treated as second class citizens for millennia. The society has been dominated by men for ages. It's high time we corrected our mistake by providing reservation to women in politics and other fields, and did justice with them.

5. If reservation can be given in the name of caste, why not reservation based on gender? After all, the objective of any kind of reservation is to provide justice to the underprivileged people of the society.

6. Women candidates can understand the plight of women better. If more and more women join politics, they'll ensure that women's exploitation stops and justice prevails for them.

Against:

1. Politics is too important a field to provide reservation. Candidates should be selected on the basis of merit, not gender. If a male candidate is worthier than his female opponent, why not vote for him?

2. Let th`e public decide who they want to vote for. Why limit their options?

3. When women can compete with men in every other field, they can compete in politics as well. What is the need of reservation then?

Our suggestion: If it is important to ensure the participation of women in politics, it won't be unfair to give them limited reservation. Women in India have been treated unjustly for a long time. Let them come forward and serve the nation. A little reservation for them will do more good than harm. However, people must take care that they always choose a worthy candidate, who could be a woman or man. If reservation, in any manner, hampers the development of the nation, it should not be there. Providing reservation to women will be like an experiment whose results will come out in the later years.

42. Deforestation

Deforestation is the process of cutting down the trees of an area for agricultural, construction, or commercial purposes. It has been stated that more than 33% of the natural forests on earth have been destroyed due to human activities. As the population explosion and urbanisation happen, people cut the trees down to clear the land for creating habitats and facilities. If the process goes on, it will endanger the environment of earth. The worst effects of deforestation are the following:

1. Trees use up carbon dioxide and release oxygen. If the trees are cut down, there'll be less oxygen in the atmosphere while the quantity of carbon dioxide will increase. This will affect the

health of the human beings and animals, and the respiratory problems will increase. Fresh air will become scarce.

2. More carbon dioxide means more heat in the atmosphere, because carbon dioxide traps solar heat and keeps it in the atmosphere. This means more global warming and high temperatures. Global warming directly affects the climate of the earth. Droughts in some areas and floods in others are some effects of global warming. (Discussed in detail in the topic 'Global Warming'.)

3. Since the roots of the trees hold the soil firmly in their place, they prevent soil erosion. When there'll be no trees, large amounts of soil will be displaced by rivers, floods and winds. This way deforestation adds to the problem of soil erosion.

4. Forests provide us with a number of useful things, including medicinal plants, wood, latex (used in the production of natural rubber), and food products (honey, fruits, etc.). Due to deforestation, we are losing this treasure.

5. Trees maintain the fertility of the soil by preventing the nutrients present in it to get washed away with rain water. Deforestation causes soil to lose these nutrients.

6. Many animal species exist only in the forests. By taking away their natural habitats, the human beings make thousands of such species extinct every year.

7. Deforestation causes increase in the area of deserts throughout the world.

8. Trees add to the plush greenery of a country and attract tourism. Thousands of tourists go to Africa because it's a green continent. Deforestation makes a country unattractive to the tourists.

Solutions to this problem:

1. Stop unauthorised cutting of trees.
2. Replace the cut trees with the new plants.
3. Find the new ways to balance human development and preservation of forests.
4. Punish those who are behind the unauthorised cutting of trees.

43. Domestic Violence

Domestic violence has been a major social problem. When we think of domestic violence, the first picture that comes to our mind is of a lady being tortured by her husband, but domestic violence can be in many forms, such as beating or abusing a child, threatening a family member, keeping an elderly person locked inside, torturing a bride for dowry, etc. Domestic violence has poisoned our nation since centuries. Some of the causes of domestic violence are the following:

1. Dowry is a major cause. When a woman does not fulfil the demands of dowry made by her in-laws and husband, she is beaten, abused and sometimes tortured and burned (and it happens not only in the poor or less educated families, but also in the rich and educated ones!).
2. Alcoholism is another major cause. A person loses the understanding of right and wrong after he is too drunk. People come home drunk and beat up their family members for paltry reasons or no reason at all.
3. Sometimes, women are beaten up for minor reasons, such as when they don't cook on time or when they refuse to bow to the demands of their husbands or in-laws (may be because the in-laws treat the bride as an outsider and not as a family member). Another reason is that in the historic times, women were treated as 'servants to their husbands'. They developed the tendency

to bear domestic violence because they believed it was God's wish and that they should always surrender to their husbands' demands. It may sound like an outdated mentality but it is still alive in many backward regions.

4. Sometimes, women are beaten up for absurd reasons, such as their failure to produce male children, or their inability to work as much as is expected from them, or for not giving 'proper respect' to the house's elders. There can be several reasons, most of them irrational.

5. Even in many of the so-called 'forward' urban families, women are beaten up for not taking proper care of the kids, for not following the family values, for not cooking well, for dowry, etc. (perhaps because drinking is prevalent in the cities too).

6. People beat their children up because of several reasons – not studying hard, not getting good marks, not being obedient, not being disciplined, not doing as told to, etc. (Sometimes, children are beaten up in schools too!). Sometimes, children are beaten so violently that they die or commit suicide.

7. Although our culture encourages us to take care of the elderly people, but the elderly people are beaten up or abused in many families. Many people treat their old parents as burdens, a hurdle in the way of their progress (or fun). They lock them inside a room; they beat or push them; they abuse them; they don't provide them eatable food or water; they don't provide them warm clothing in winter (not because they can't afford it, but because they don't want to 'waste' money on it).

8. In many recent cases, women have been found beating their husbands or children. All these are the forms of domestic violence.

What can be done about it:

1. The best and permanent solutions are the social ones. If a society resolves not to let domestic violence happen in any house, it can stop such incidences. Those who commit the acts of violence, may be boycotted or embarrassed for their actions. The elderly people of the society must make it an unofficial (or official) rule not to let any form of domestic violence happen. Half the problem can be solved this way. The victims should be made aware of their rights. They can always take police's help if nothing else works.

2. Another solution is legal solution. The person who commits the acts of violence and doesn't reform, may be arrested and punished. If necessary, a lawsuit may follow.

3. The NGOs can (and do) play a very vital role in stopping the domestic violence. The women's rights activists and child protection organisations should come forward and protect the victim. The victim should be courageous enough to go and report the acts of violence to the police or such NGOs. If the victim is a child, the neighbours should report such incidences to the police or NGOs.

4. The mentality that women are a weak gender must change. That will be the permanent solution to the problem of domestic violence against them.

Our suggestion: Domestic violence will not remain a big problem if the whole society decides to act against it. The government has also run awareness campaigns against domestic violence (Do you remember the TV ads in which a neighbour comes and presses the doorbell when a husband is beating his wife?). A society cannot be called a civilised society unless the domestic violence is eradicated completely.

44. Dowry System in India – Should We Get Rid of It?

In favour of dowry:

Nothing.

Against dowry system:

1. Dowry is the reason behind the murders of many brides. The in-laws demand more and more dowry, and when they don't get it, they torture the bride or even kill her. Some brides are burned alive for dowry!

2. The dowry system compels the parents of the girls to save money for years, and then give that money away as dowry. They give their daughter and they give money as well. This doesn't sound like justice, does it? (Especially when many girls are able to work and earn money.)

3. Because of the dowry system, the cases of female foeticide have increased, because people believe it's painful to have a girl child, as they'll have to save money for her dowry.

4. The concept of dowry itself is against the human values, because it obviously makes a girl look like a second-class human being, who has to be given away with a pile of money to the other family. It definitely goes against the self-esteem of a girl.

5. When poor people can't amass 'sufficient' dowry money, they become the victims of the society's cruel laughter and disgust. So become the brides from the poor families among their in-laws.

6. Demanding or offering dowry is against law. It should not be done. (However, there are often loopholes in the laws and people take advantages of them.)

7. Sometimes, the dowry laws are misused against the groom's family. If we eradicate the dowry system, there'll be no need of such laws too.

8. Some parents argue that they are only giving gifts to their daughter; and may be, there's nothing wrong with that. But they must take care not to fulfil any unjustifiable demands of the groom's family, as by doing that, they might endanger their own daughter's happiness (or life) because greed knows no end.

What can be done about dowry system:

1. If a girl is being tortured for dowry, she should seek the help of police or women rights organisations ASAP. She should also tell her parents.
2. If the groom's family has demanded dowry before the marriage itself, the bride's family should not make the foolish mistake of marrying her into that greedy family.
3. The society should report any incidence of dowry to the police.

Our suggestion: We should abolish the dowry system as soon as possible because this outdated system is against the human values and the law. There can be no justification to it.

45. The Commonwealth

The Commonwealth (or simply Commonwealth) is the group of independent nations that were part of the British Empire in the past. In total, there are 54 commonwealth nations at present (only 2 of them were not a part of the British Empire). Some dependencies of the commonwealth nations are also a part of the Commonwealth. Some of the commonwealth nations are Australia, India, Pakistan, Bangladesh, New Zealand, Singapore, Kenya, South Africa, etc. Queen Elizabeth II is the head of the Commonwealth. The major objectives of the Commonwealth are to fight the poverty spread in the member nations, to end racism, to promote world peace and democracy, and to boost free trade between its members. But many people know the Commonwealth because of the Commonwealth Games, which are held every four years. In 2010, these games were held in Delhi *(details in the next topic)*. The Commonwealth games are the third largest sports event in the world (after Olympics and Asian Games).

46. Delhi Commonwealth Games, 2010

In October 2010, Delhi hosted the 19th Commonwealth Games. It was one of the biggest sports events ever held in India. 71 nations participated in these games. Australia topped the medal tally with 74 gold medals while the host India stood second with 38 gold medals. Some of the stars from the Indian side were Gagan Narang (shooting), Saina Nehwal (Badminton), Anisa Sayyed (shooting), Omkar Singh (shooting), Abhinav Bindra (shooting), Susheel Kumar (wrestling), etc. Shera, a friendly tiger, the mascot of these games, became popular in the Commonwealth.

More than the games themselves, what brought more publicity to the games were apprehensions about the games. When the athletes from the other countries reached India, some of them found that their accommodations in the Commonwealth village were not ready and they were accommodated in various hotels. Some reporters were not sure whether the stadiums would be ready by the time the games commenced. People doubted whether the games could be taken away from India because of the delays in the preparation of stadiums. But after the spectacular opening ceremony of the games, all the apprehensions vanished and the national and international media praised the ceremony. The events took place on time and the games finished with a nice closing ceremony. It is said that the success of the commonwealth games increased the chances of India winning an Olympic Games bid (while the initial delays had reduced those chances).

The Commonwealth Games scam (CWG scam) was another thing that drew the attention of the people. Some of the top officials were accused of being indulged in corrupt practices, and the cases against them are still going on in the courts.

The Commonwealth Games helped highlight Delhi and India on the world map. They also displayed India's rising impact in the world.

47. Cricket – A Game or A Religion?

Cricket as a game:

Cricket is, undoubtedly, the most popular sport in India. Though it is not the national game of India, it can be compared with what Football is to Brazil and Karate is to Japan. When few people were able to afford TV sets, people used to listen to the umpires' commentaries on the radio sets, and used to gather around the TV shops. In a way, cricket has helped unite India. No matter whether people from different states know each other's language or not, they enjoy cricket together. They all rejoice when Sachin Tendulkar makes a century and when Virender Sehwag scores a six. There have been some moments of pride in the history of India when the country won the Cricket World Cup (twice, in 1983 and in 2011) and the 20-20 World Cup (in 2007). All these moments were celebrated like Diwali or New Year. Some of the finest athletes of India are cricketers. Cricket has also helped highlight India on the world map.

Cricket – a religion?

While cricket is prospering in India, other games are perhaps being forgotten because people do not pay enough attention to them. It has happened many times that the medal winners of other games were found to be waiting for taxi or auto because the sports officials didn't make arrangements for them. Some of the senior hockey players work at the railway platforms; some athletes never get enough compensation to fulfil their basic needs; the stadiums of other games are often found in pitiful conditions. While some people may not want to believe it, but overemphasis on only one game can be a contributor to such a situation. Under such conditions, how can India win more medals in Olympics, the biggest sports event in the world?

When India loses (or is about to lose) a cricket match, some people start throwing water bottles and garbage in the cricket stadiums, because they cannot see the Indian team lose a match. They forget that Cricket is a game. This shows poor game spirit and is not good for the image of our nation.

Even the cricketers suffer when people make this game a religion. When India loses an important cricket match to Pakistan, or when the Indian team loses many matches in a series, people gather outside the cricketers' houses and protest; sometimes, they even burn their effigies. Is that what we should do to the people who play for our nation?

Some people have accused Cricket of taking away the limelight from the other important events taking place in the country. It has been noticed that many media channels show news related to Cricket for a long time even if a major incident has taken place. Why does this happen? Because people want to see Cricket and its news more and more.

Our suggestion: Cricket is a wonderful game and it has done a lot for India. But it should not become a religion. We should treat it as a game. Of course, it is not Cricket's fault, but people's fault that they let their emotions get over them. It will be good for the nation and good for Cricket as well, if we can enjoy it with game spirit.

48. India's Olympic Dreams

Olympic games are the world's largest sports event. Thousands of athletes from all over the world participate in them. India has two kinds of dreams associated with the Olympic games – 1) To win lots of gold medals in Olympics, 2) To host Olympic games in India. Usually, people talk about the former when they talk about India's Olympic dreams. Also, whether India will host Olympic games in the coming years also depends on how many gold medals the Indians win in Olympic games (a senior member of the International Olympic Committee had said this during an interview).

India has long dreamed of Olympic gold medals, but it has not won too many so far. In fact, India has only won one individual Olympic gold medal (Abhinav Bindra in 2008) and 8 team gold medals (in Hockey), thus, nine Olympic gold medals till 2008 (while Michael Phelps, the famous swimmer, has alone won 14 Olympic golds in two different Olympics). India, the country which accounts for around 17% population of the world, has a poor record in Olympic games. The major reasons behind the poor performance of our athletes are these:

1. Lack of quality training and training facilities. The Indian athletes do not get the required facilities and equipment to train for Olympic games. Even the top athletes complain of the lack of facilities sometimes. Without high-level training, it may not be possible for an athlete to win an Olympic gold.

2. India lacks infrastructure for the training of the athletes. There are too few stadiums; and the ones which are there, are not in a very good condition.

3. Many Indian athletes do not get enough financial support to train and to live. They need to divide their time between training and earning for their families. It is difficult to maintain a balance between the two.

4. India has never been a country too enthusiastic about sports (Cricket being an exception). Most people focus only on studies, and they treat sports as a secondary activity. This indifferent attitude towards sports has never allowed India to become a sports heaven for the athletes.

Unless these drawbacks are removed, India is less likely to win enough gold medals to satisfy the thirst of the nation.

Now, talking about hosting Olympic games. It requires great deal of efforts to host Olympic games. The host city has to have a good reputation and great infrastructure. Even here we have some limitations:

1. Infrastructure is a major concern of the Indian Olympic Association. The power sources, transport facilities, security services, airports, all need to be upgraded for Olympic games. We need to create more five-star hotels to accommodate thousands of tourists, who come to watch Olympics.
2. We do not have good enough stadiums or training facilities. Many international athletes, who have high demands, may refuse to come and play unless they're sure they'll get all they want here.
3. The Indian athletes will have to win more gold medals to prove that our facilities are good enough to produce gold winners.
4. A lot of diplomatic efforts are needed to be made at the international level to convince the international community about our capabilities to host Olympics. Diplomacy plays an important role in every field.
5. When Olympic games were held in Beijing, the people of the city were given proper training for how they should behave with the tourists. Same needs to be done here.
6. During the 2010 Commonwealth games, the stadiums remained empty during many sports events. Why would the athletes want to play when there are no viewers to watch and motivate them? People will have to show enough enthusiasm for the games. Moreover, they will have to have money to buy expensive tickets! (Though now crores of Indians are earning well and this should not be a big deal for them to buy Olympic tickets.)
7. Money is crucial when it comes to hosting big events. Olympics are very expensive events. India, a developing nation, will have to spend a lot of money to host these games.

49. Public Transport in the Indian Cities

Why people should use public transport instead of their own vehicles:

1. Using public transport helps us preserve our fossil fuels. Think how much petrol and diesel will be saved if people start using buses and metros instead of cars!

2. Using public transport is much cheaper than using own cars and bikes. A person can save a lot of money on petrol or diesel if he or she starts using public transport.

3. When more and more people use buses and trains, there'll be fewer cars on the road. There'll be fewer traffic jams, and it will save everybody's time.

4. Using public transport helps reduce air pollution. Fewer vehicles on the road mean less smoke. This will be great not only for the environment, but also for the health of the people.

5. When everyone's using public transport, the country will save a lot of money it spends on buying petroleum from other countries.

6. Using public transport is good for the society. When people commute together, they talk to each other, they discuss the national issues, and they share problems with each other. They also make good friends.

Why, then, people do not use public transport:

1. Our buses, trains and metros are often overcrowded; especially in the office hours. People do not get seats. Who would like to travel standing everyday? It's all very uncomfortable.

2. Buses and trains often run late. Sometimes, people have to skip a bus because it's tightly packed. Who would like to get late to the office? Cars and bikes move faster, as they don't have to stop on every stop. That's why people prefer them.

3. People have to take extra precautions in buses and trains, as their belongings may get stolen. There are many pick-pockets, who are looking for people's hard-earned money.

4. Buses and trains are often littered with garbage. People avoid travelling in the dirty compartments.

5. Public transport does not take people to the doorsteps of their destinations. When you use a bus, you have to get down at the bus stop nearest to your destination, while your own car/bike can be taken inside the building. (Hey, it's good for health to walk a few blocks everyday!)

6. Eve-teasing is a problem in public transport. That's why women prefer their own cars.

Our suggestion: Using public transport is the need of the hour. In order to motivate people to use public transport, some concrete steps are needed to be taken. Government will have to arrange more number of buses and train-coaches to meet the demands of our large population. In addition, buses and trains must be kept clean, they should arrive on time, and there should be more number of security personnel to protect the people from the criminals.

50. Preserving Our Historical Monuments

Why is it important:

1. Historical monuments (old forts, statues, buildings, etc.) are the signs of our thousands of years old history and culture. They state how rich our past had been. They must be preserved because they are historically extremely important and help the students and scholars understand our history.

2. Historical monuments attract tourists and help thousands of Indians earn their living. Thousands of tourists visit them every year. In fact, it has been found that it is the historical monuments of India, and not the recent development, which attract most of the tourists. Therefore, they are economically important too.

3. When a tourist visits these monuments, he takes their pictures with him and shows them to other people. This way he spreads the knowledge of the Indian history and culture. Therefore, our monuments must be preserved.

How to preserve them:

1. We should fine the culprits, who write on them or scratch them
2. We should create awareness about the importance of historical monuments and how they help people earn their living.
3. We should reduce the level of pollution around them.
4. We should not let any illegal construction take place near them. Such constructions loosen the soil holding the monuments.

Our suggestion: Historical monuments are the living treasures from our past. They must be preserved because nothing can replace them.

51. Security of Women in the Indian Cities

There has been an increase in the number of crimes against women (rapes, molestation, eve-teasing, murder after rape, chain-snatching, purse snatching, etc.) in the Indian cities; at least, the media reports suggest so. Women do not feel safe because of these incidences. They fear living/travelling/commuting to work alone. These incidences are taking place at an alarming rate, even in the posh areas. In fact, many such cases are not even reported because many victims fear possible defamation. Even the female tourists are feeling the sting of crimes. There have been incidences of rapes with foreigners at some tourist destinations. Eve-teasers are another problem. Women are losing faith in law and security. Sometimes, even the security guards are involved in the crimes. Women and children are often considered to be the soft target. To make the situation worse, rich and powerful criminals believe they can escape the law.

What should be done:

1. There must be better security arrangements for women in the crime-sensitive areas of our cities. More number of policemen must be deployed there.

2. More number of police vans must patrol the city roads.

3. Efforts should be made to make the police more trustworthy and friendly. This will encourage the women to report the incidences of crime.

4. Women should be trained in Martial Arts and self-defence tactics. They must be taught the use of pepper-sprays.

5. Rapists and molesters must be punished hard, no matter how powerful or rich they are. They must not be allowed to escape the law.

6. Women rights activists and NGOs can play important roles in such cases. They should support the victim and assist her in the law procedure.

7. Women can commute in groups whenever possible.

8. We can reserve some coaches and seats for women in the trains, metros and buses. Special buses may be run for them. (Delhi metro has some coaches reserved for women.)

9. Men must be encouraged to come forward and help a victim if a crime is taking place. They must be assured that they will not be drawn into lengthy legal procedures.

Our suggestion: Women had been compared with God in our ancient scriptures. Security of women (and children) shows how safe and civilized a society is. If women don't feel safe, the image of the country suffers. Therefore, we must do everything possible to ensure the security of women in our cities.

52. Ethics in Business – Why Are They Important?

1. A business without ethics is like a life without values. Nobody trusts a businessman, who doesn't follow any ethical values; his customers do not trust him and his partners can't trust him; even the employees can't trust their bosses in such a business. What if the business owner takes people's money and runs away, without delivering the promised goods or services? And how many times can such a business fool the customers? Only once. A business without ethics will sink sooner or later.

2. In order to get full dedication and commitment of its employees, a business must follow some ethical values. If a business organisation is just opportunistic, the employees will tend to get away as soon as their personal goals (ethical or unethical) are achieved. For instance, if the employees know that their bosses are deceiving the customer somehow, they'll themselves think about gaining a share of the loot and get away with it. Moreover, it is quite natural that the people who work for ethical, and hence esteemed, organizations have higher levels of satisfaction, self-respect and commitment because they know they are working for something worthwhile.

3. A business that doesn't follow ethical practices is bound to get into trouble sooner or later. On the other hand, a business that follows ethical values will attract public's support and goodwill, even if someone files a lawsuit against it.

4. Anyone involved in unethical business practices undergoes high levels of stress because he fears being caught.

Our suggestion: Ethics play a very important role in any business. It is true that you can't fool the customers or your partners for a long time. Even law cannot take the place of ethics because law cannot punish a person until he has committed a crime and it has been proved. People trust a business because of its clean track record and the ethical values it follows; not because there's a law to punish the guilty, because no law has a success rate of one-hundred percent.

53. Family or Career?

(Note: When asked randomly, most people say 'family' and a few say 'career'. But in a discussion, you have to be on the safe side. If you say family, people may think you have no ambition, and if you say career, people may think you are either lying or you are too ambitious to enjoy the social life.)

Arguments in favour of the family:

1. What will a great career mean to a person if he has lost support of his family in pursuit of success; or worse, if he no longer has a family to enjoy his success with him? Families fall apart when people don't give enough attention to their wives and children.
2. A person needs wholehearted support of his family to achieve a great success in his career. If the family doesn't support a person, he may not reach the altitudes he wants to.
3. Why do people want to achieve success? In many cases, for their families!

Arguments in favour of the career:

1. Every family wants its members to have successful careers. In most cases, happiness of a family is directly attached to the success of its members.
2. It is a bitter truth that people who do not have successful careers might not get the expected respect in their families (or at least they might feel so). Therefore, success in career is crucial for an individual.
3. People who are successful in their careers are often happy in life, and only happy people can keep their families happy.

Our suggestion: Family and career, both are important in a person's life. What a person needs to do is strike a balance between the pursuit of success in his career and happiness of his family. Only a person who has both, a happy family and a shining career, can be called a successful person.

54. Time Management

Time has become the scarcest commodity in the present world. A person needs to divide his time between various tasks. He needs to take care of his career, take his family on a vacation, and spend time with his friends too. A student needs to allocate time to studies, friendly gossips, sports, and his family. Only a few people can achieve this balance; most people lag behind in one or two areas. This makes effective time management so important. One should be able to get the maximum benefit of the hours available to him.

How to manage time:

1. Prioritise the tasks: A person who knows his priorities will not leave the most important tasks for the last moment. What is more important must be done first.

2. Drop the burden: It is very important not to waste time in fruitless activities; especially when there is limited time available for the important ones. It may not be a good idea to watch a late night movie when you have to get up early next morning to catch a train.

3. Doing the activities in their prime hours: You may not be able to focus on studies as good in the noisy evening hours as in the quiet early morning hours. Similarly, you may not take interest in playing in the afternoon hours when the sun is at its peak. It is very important to allot the most appropriate hours to each important activity. It saves time because what you can do in fifteen minutes in its prime hours can take an hour when done in the wrong hours.

4. Doing the physical and mental activities alternatively: You should play when you are mentally exhausted after your studies, and you

should study when you are physically exhausted after playing. This is how we can make the best use of time, by alternating the physical activities with the mental ones.

5. Concept of 'quality time' is very important to understand. A person may spend hours with his wife, watching a movie but thinking about office work all the time, while all he must do is take a ten-minute walk with her at the lake-side or in a garden. It may be better to spend little but quality time with your family instead of spending long hours with diverted attention. Your family understands your problems.

6. It is good to involve your family in your work, if and wherever possible. That way they'll be able to understand your challenges better.

7. Someone said it is better to sharpen your axe before you go and cut a tree. What he meant is that you should recharge yourself before you start a work. It may be a good idea to take a nice, one-week vacation after a long, tiring year before you begin the next year's works.

55. What is More Important – Process or Result?

In favour of result:

1. All is well that ends well. It is said that a person forgets all the pain he has suffered during the process if he gets good results. A student may forget the painful hours he has put into tough studies if he gets good marks in the end-term exams. An athlete may forget all the pains of training if he wins the competition he prepared so hard for. Therefore, result is more important.

2. Why do we do anything? To get the desired results! Results are surely very important.

In favour of process:

1. Result is momentary; process is long. If the process has been too painful, even sweet results may not justify the pain. For instance, if a person has worked hard all his life, trying to earn more and more money, but has not enjoyed sufficient time with his family during the lengthy process, all his money may not compensate for the time gone; worse if he developed a disease by not paying attention to his health!

2. If the process has been sweet, it may even compensate for sore results sometimes. For instance, if a teacher has enjoyed a wonderful lifetime teaching his students, he may not regret that he could have taken a high paying job in the corporate.

3. Will it be good for a nation if it develops at the cost of poor people living in it? Will that development be justified? No. The nation will have to design the process in such a manner that it considers the benefit of both the rich and the poor. This too shows that the process (of development) is as important as the result (development) itself.

4. Even the result depends on the process. If the process is not correct, we may not get the desired result. For example, if a student wastes time, he may not get good marks (because the process has been faulty). How is the process less important than the end result, then?

Our suggestion: Process is as important as result. To get the desired results, we must focus our efforts on the process.

56. Pollution in Our Rivers – What to Do About It? (or 'How to Save the Ganges, Our Sacred River?')

Our rivers have been polluted since ages. The pollution has become so intense that there are very few rivers whose water can be consumed directly without falling ill. Some of the largest rivers have been turned into dumping sites at places.

Where does the pollution come from and what we should do about it:

1. Industrial garbage and chemicals (dyes and others) are dumped directly into the rivers, without treating or neutralising them first. These chemicals are hazardous to human health, marine animal species and plants at the banks of rivers. Dumping of chemicals must be stopped immediately, and the water coming out of the factories must be treated before it enters the river stream.

2. At many places, sewerage water enters the rivers directly. Along it brings billions of bacteria and viruses. This must stop immediately. Sewerage water must be treated in the water treatment plants before it enters the stream.

3. In some states, people immerse God's idols into the rivers. Many of these idols are painted with harmful colours, paints and dyes. Such material should not be used in painting the idols.

4. People should not use soaps and shampoos when they bathe in the rivers.

5. There must be a complete ban on dumping of polythene and plastic bags into the rivers. Plastic takes years to degrade completely.

6. Some species of fish are known to clean the river water. They consume algae and fungus. In order to fight the natural pollution, these fish may be introduced into the rivers.

7. Illegal constructions at the banks of the rivers must be stopped. They hamper the free flow of the stream.

Our suggestion: Many ancient civilisations had originated or developed on the banks of the rivers. The rivers provide us drinking water and irrigation water, and we produce electricity using the force of streams. It is our duty to keep our rivers clean.

57. Air Pollution in India

Air pollution has become a big problem in India, especially in the cities. Clean air is everyone's requirement, but it has become more like a luxury. People visit natural tourist destinations to enjoy pure air. Air pollution directly affects the health of all the living beings. Polluted air causes a number of respiratory diseases. The major causes of air pollution and their solutions are as follows:

1. Chimneys of the factories release a lot of untreated smoke into the air. This smoke contains carbon and other industrial pollutants. This smoke must be treated using electrostatic precipitators or other devices before it is released into the air. Moreover, chimneys must be tall enough to release the smoke at a higher altitude.

2. Automobiles also release a lot of pollutants in the air. They must be thoroughly checked before they are given 'Pollution Under Control (PUC)' certificate. People should use more of public transport.

3. Smoking at public places must stop. Laws against smoking at public places must be enforced effectively.

4. People should avoid using firecrackers (or they must use them in minimum quantities) on any festival and New Year celebration.

5. More trees must be planted. They help reduce air pollution. They also emit oxygen.

6. Compressed Natural Gas (CNG) must be used instead of petrol and diesel in the automobiles wherever possible. It has been a very successful formula in Delhi and some other cities.

7. Waste that smells foul must not be collected in the open.

Our suggestion: By taking some precautionary measures, we can significantly reduce the level of pollution in the air.

58. Terrorism in India

The problem of terrorism is now a global one. Terrorism has struck in almost every part of the world. 9/11 attacks on the World Trade Centre in the USA, attacks on the Spanish trains, attacks on the Tube stations in London, attacks in the cities of Russia, Baghdad, Bali and Pakistan are some examples of worldwide terrorism. Perhaps there's no nation where the terrorists have not attacked. Unfortunately, India has been one of the biggest victims of terrorism. The terrorists have attacked the Indian Parliament, India's financial capital, Mumbai and many other cities (Jaipur, Pune, Hyderabad, Bangalore, etc.). Jammu and Kashmir has been the biggest victim of terrorism among the Indian states. It has been estimated that more than 60,000 people in Jammu and Kashmir have lost their lives to terrorism.

What should be done to fight terrorism in India:

1. Internal security of the big Indian cities must be upgraded. Sensitive places must be guarded heavily, and the anti-terrorism units must be provided better weapons and communication equipment and bullet-proof dresses. More National Security Guard (NSG) units must be kept near the industrial areas and big cities.

2. People should be trained to act promptly whenever they see any suspicious thing or person. They must not touch that thing and inform the police immediately.

3. India should use its diplomatic options wisely. We should convince the international community to put pressure on Pakistan to stop the terror activities from its soil. We should make sure that the money which Pakistan is receiving in the name of international aid must not be used to support terror against India. If Pakistan doesn't agree, we should severe our economic ties with Pakistan. As a last resort, India must keep the option of attacking the terrorist camps across the border open (since it may lead to full scale war or even a nuclear war, it can only be the last option).

4. Satellite technology may be used to keep track of the terrorist activities across the border.

5. We should guard our international borders more heavily in order to prevent the terrorists from entering the nation. Our intelligence should be made more effective.

6. India is seen as a soft target by the terrorists. This image should change. Those involved in the terror activities should be punished hard and without delay.

Our suggestion: Terrorism can only stop when there is a better coordination between the people and the security agencies, because the security agencies can't be everywhere all the time but people can be. It is everyone's duty to take a firm stand against terrorism.

59. Corruption in India

Corruption is a burning issue these days. Every other day we hear about scams like 2G, CWG, Tehelka revelation, Bofors, Mining Scams and what not. The nation has been rattled by scams. And then there's day-to-day corruption in various offices. All this has put India in the list of the most corrupt countries in the world.

Causes of corruption in India:

1. Blind chase for money leads to corruption. Since everyone wants everything, people don't mind paying bribe to get *their* works done before others'. Ethics have taken a back seat due to the cut-throat competition.

2. Red-tape provides room for corruption at various levels. The processes in India are lengthy, cumbersome and less transparent. No one knows what goes on behind the curtains. People pay bribes to get their urgent works done.

3. Failure of our judiciary to provide timely justice in the corruption cases has become a motivating factor for the people involved in the corrupt practices. They know they will not be harmed until the case is done (and that may take years). Therefore, the common man finds it easier to pay bribe than to go to the courts.

4. The population of India is so huge that many people find it wiser to pay bribes and get the work done than to wait in long queues for the simple works.

5. Many people are unaware of their rights and duties. They don't know whether they have options other than paying bribe. They don't understand it's their duty not to pay bribes. Illiteracy is the problem behind it.

6. Due to petty reasons (such as regionalism, casteism, religionism, etc.), people vote for unworthy candidates, whose only motive is to come into the power and earn as much as they can through corruption.

What can be done about corruption:

1. Fast-track courts must be set up to solve the corruption and scam cases.

2. Awareness must be created among the people. They must know their rights and duties. They must be made aware about the 'Right to Information' Act (RTI).

3. Licensing and other processes must be made more transparent and less cumbersome.

4. People should elect the right representatives who will work for the nation rather than their own benefits.

5. Ethics education and training should be provided to the students, employees, officers and the elected representatives of the people.

6. The business leaders should come forward and tell the people how corruption is weakening our economy day-by-day.

Our suggestion: It is a duty of every Indian to raise his or her voice against corruption. Efforts of a few people cannot defeat corruption; the whole nation will have to come together to root out this problem.

60. Artificial Intelligence – Can It Replace Human Intelligence?

Artificial intelligence refers to smart machines and computer programs which can help the humans make rational decisions based on the data provided to them. They often use mathematical algorithms to do so. They can do the things that the human beings consider intelligent (such as suggesting stocks by analysing the stock market data, playing chess, counting, identifying objects, etc.). Some of the things these machines and programs can do are considered tough for the human beings. For example, a computer takes seconds to do the calculations and analyses that otherwise will take hours or even days for the human beings to do. Artificial intelligence is being used in various fields – medical (example: using robotic arms to perform operations), Quantitative Analysis, communication (example: smart phones), manufacturing (example- to determine the compositions of constituents of a liquid), finance (counting notes), wars (unmanned planes and heat-seeking missiles), business (using RFID to order and replenish items on the shelf), space exploration being some of them. Some people believe that artificial intelligence can possibly replace human intelligence in many or all of the fields. But can it really do so? Let us consider some facts:

1. Machines have no emotions. They can only provide the solutions based on the data we provide to them but they cannot take the decisions in which emotions are (or have to be) involved. For instance, a wounded soldier would not want a robot to treat him, because the machine will show no emotions even if the person

is crying in pain. Similarly, a robot soldier will only shoot the enemy, without showing mercy to even those who deserve it.

2. Machines can only work as they are programmed. They will not think of the welfare of the person using them. They will not show dedication towards work; they will not work overtime unless ordered to do so; they may not consider the changes taking place around them before reaching a decision (For instance, a smart machine can tell you which stock is a good bargain, but it can't tell you whether the company will survive another year).
3. Intelligence of machines is quite limited. They cannot even see the obvious sometimes. For instance, a machine can count the number of customers entering a shop, but it can't tell whether it was the same customer, who entered the shop four times. A computer can beat a player in chess, but it cannot decide whether it should play chess.
4. Machines have no ethical values.

Our suggestion: Artificial Intelligence cannot (and must not!) replace human intelligence, but it can definitely help a human being live a better life. It can help us take better decisions for our own future.

61. Indo-US Nuclear Deal

India-US nuclear deal is a civil nuclear agreement between USA and India. It was declared in 2005 and 2006 and became operational in October 2008 when the representatives from both the countries signed the deal. It is also called '123 Agreement'. India strongly needed this deal because it ensures that India will keep getting nuclear fuel (Uranium and other radioactive material) for its nuclear reactors. These reactors provide the energy needed for the civil purposes. Besides providing access to the nuclear fuel, the deal enables India to exchange the related technology with the USA and other countries. This technology can be used in various fields such as agriculture, weather forecasting and health, etc.

The salient features of the deal are:

1. The deal enables India and the US to trade nuclear material and equipment required for civil purposes. This will ensure that India doesn't fall short of the nuclear material required for its nuclear reactors. The deal also allows India to keep a reserve of nuclear fuel. India can also reprocess the utilised nuclear material if it needs to.
2. In case the supply of nuclear fuel still disrupts due to any reason, India and the USA will work together with other nations (Russia, the UK, France, etc.) to restore the supply.
3. Besides the nuclear fuel, both the countries can work together in the fields of nuclear research, reactor designing, construction, operation and maintenance, etc.
4. The US reserves the right to demand the return of the provided nuclear fuel and technology.

India's good non-proliferation record helped secure this deal with the US.

The deal faced certain amount of opposition in India. While the left parties accused that the deal would negatively affect India's independent foreign policy, the opposition stated that by signing the deal India would sacrifice its right to conduct more nuclear tests, though the government disagreed.

Some of the countries which supported the deal were Russia, the UK, France, Germany, Japan, while some countries extended their support later on. Pakistan and China expressed concerns over the deal.

62. Should India Sign CTBT?

CTBT stands for **C**omprehensive Nuclear **T**est **B**an **T**reaty (or simply Comprehensive Test Ban Treaty). This treaty calls for a ban on all the nuclear tests, in atmosphere, under water or underground, for any purpose. Many countries have signed the treaty while many others have not. Among those which have signed the treaty are Russia, the US, China, the UK and France and others (not all these countries have ratified the treaty yet). Some of the countries which have not signed the treaty yet are India, Pakistan, North Korea, Israel, Iran, etc. Though India supports the ban on nuclear explosions (India's first PM, Pt. Jawaharlal Nehru, was among the first leaders who advocated a ban on nuclear tests), but it has some genuine concerns.

Why India hasn't signed CTBT:

1. CTBT does not take into account the existing stockpile of the nuclear weapons of various countries. India has very few nuclear weapons when compared to the USA, Russia and China.

2. No time limit has been set for the nuclear disarmament in this treaty. It only focuses on non-proliferation.

3. India has not been included into the club of the Nuclear States yet. The official nuclear states get some unstated advantages due to some obligations of the treaty.

4. Some Indian scientists have said that India has not acquired sufficient scientific data from the Pokhran Nuclear tests and it may require some more tests. They advise the government not to sign the CTBT yet. On the other hand, many countries (including India's major competitor, China) have acquired the data they needed for their security goals by performing multiple nuclear tests. (China has conducted 43 nuclear tests and USA itself has done more than a thousand nuclear tests. In total, more than 2,000 tests have been conducted so far.)

5. Since India has already adopted the policy of 'No-first use' of nuclear weapons, it already fulfils the obligations of the treaty, though it has not signed it yet.

Our suggestion: India should not sign the CTBT unless it has sufficient nuclear data to meet its security needs. Since it is highly unlikely that the required data will be made available by the countries which have it, India may have no other option but to conduct nuclear tests in future.

63. Right To Information Act (RTI Act)

Right to Information Act, commonly called RTI, came into force in 2005 in all the Indian states except Jammu and Kashmir (where a similar but separate act was enacted). The objective of the Right to Information Act was to promote transparency in the working of the public authorities. Some of the most important features of RTI are:

1. Under the RTI Act, any citizen of India can demand information from a public authority. The information can be in the form of document, press release, record, circular, e-mail, electronic data, contract sample, etc. However, certain information may not be disclosed (such as information that may affect security and sovereignty of our nation, trade secrets, etc.).
2. Information will be provided within a period of 30 days, unless abnormal circumstances arise. If the matter is so urgent that it directly affects the life or liberty of a person, information will be provided within 48 hours.
3. Every public authority has an obligation to provide information demanded under RTI.
4. There is also a penalty for refusal to receive the application for information.

It is expected that RTI will be a powerful tool in the hands of common men to fight corruption. It was also suggested that RTI was as effective as bribes to get the work done in time. Some officers who refused to provide information were fined, and in some cases, the information was made available within days or hours. It has been found that both poor and rich are exercising this right.

Our suggestion: While RTI may not end the deep-rooted corruption alone, it will definitely give the common man a hope against corruption.

64. Agni-V

Agni-V is India's first Inter-continental Ballistic Missile (ICBM). It was developed by DRDO and was successfully test-fired in April 2012. It has a range of 5,000-6,000 kilometres, though some people believe that it has a longer range. Experts believe that India needed a long range missile to counter the threat of China's nukes and that this missile was prepared keeping China in view. India and China lack mutual trust in relations, especially since the 1962 India-China war. China has threatened India many times and has been a friend of Pakistan. China has missiles which can reach longer ranges (even more than 10,000 kms). The successful launch of Agni-V has made India a member of the group of countries, commonly called the 'elite nuclear club' (countries which have ICBMs).

While most countries of the world did not take the test-launch as a threat, reactions from China were different. One of the leading newspapers of China said that India should not 'over-estimate its strength' because it stands nowhere in the overall arms race with China. It also added that while India lags behind China in infrastructure, its society is highly supportive of developing nuclear power. China also criticized the Western countries for not taking a stand against India's ICBM test. It warned that Agni-V had a range of up to 8,000 km but India deliberately downplayed the missile's capability.

Among other reactions, an expert from the USA said that the US was familiar with India's defence needs and, therefore, it didn't mind India testing a long range missile. NATO said India's missile was no threat to it. Even Pakistan did not take a stand against the missile launch, stating that New Delhi had acted according to its agreement with Pakistan by informing the latter about the test ahead of time.

Our suggestion: India needed a long range ballistic missile to create a balance of power with China, a country which is far ahead of us in arms and missile power. Agni-V is not against any country but for peaceful purpose, as it acts as a deterrent against a nuclear attack. India is a responsible nation with a clean and proven track record of non-proliferation. Moreover, it has a 'no first use' policy. From its bitter experience with China in 1962, India has learned that it needs to have sufficient power to counter any threat from a powerful nation. That's why India needed Agni-V.

65. We Need Food for Everyone, Not Missile (or 'Missile or Infrastructure?')

Some people say that instead of spending millions on the development of missiles and other weapons, India should spend its money to feed its poor people. They argue that a large part of India's population lives below poverty line and it needs food more than missiles. They say that India doesn't have a good infrastructure, sufficient number of schools and hospitals, and sufficient electricity to fulfil the needs of its population, then why doesn't India spend more on these basic needs instead of spending on missiles?

The answer is that we just cannot ignore our defence needs. Can we forget what happened in 1962, when our soldiers fought with outdated weapons against the Chinese soldiers who had better weapons? No. We also wouldn't want to imagine what would have happened if India hadn't had better weapons in the wars of 1965 and 1971. The real question is – Can you live in a house which has everything you need, except proper security? No. Such house will not defend you against the thieves and your enemies. Similarly, India cannot afford to spend all its money on the basic needs of its population and spend nothing on the research and development of missiles. We have to, even if we don't want to, because we have no choice! Can those people, who criticise India's missile program, guarantee that India will never be attacked in future? No, they can't! There's no country in the world that can live in peace without fulfilling its defence needs.

India will have to maintain a balance between expenditure on its defence needs and expenditure on the basic needs of its population.

Only then India will have both – peace and prosperity. May be we will never have to strike any nation with a nuclear capable missile, but still we will have to develop them to keep the enemy away from our land.

66. High Oil Prices – What Can People Do About It?

India imports a lot of oil from other nations to meet the demands of its population. In other words, India spends billions of dollars on importing oil every year. Since India is not one of the big oil producers, it has no control over the oil prices in the international market. The oil prices keep fluctuating. Sometimes, they are below \$100/barrel and, sometimes, they touch the \$140/barrel mark (according to the data obtained between 2007 and 2012).

When the oil prices shoot up, the prices of many commodities in India tend to go up, because the transportation charges increase too. Besides, people need petrol and diesel to run their vehicles. What should then the people do about the hikes in oil prices? Well, here's what a common man can do:

1. We should try to reduce our dependence on petrol and diesel. Instead of using private vehicles every time, we should use public transport. Public transport is not only cheaper, but using it also saves a lot of money we spend on oil. No doubt, the government will have to take some concrete steps to encourage people to use public transport. Buses and trains have to be made more comfortable and clean, and they must be sufficient in number so that they don't get overcrowded. For shorter distances, people can walk or use bicycles. It improves health too.

2. Research and development are very important to reduce our dependence on oil. We, along with friendly countries, should try to develop cars and other vehicles which do not require oil to run. In some countries, solar-powered vehicles are being used for public transport. In India, we have rechargeable cars that use electricity as fuel (but they haven't become too popular

yet). People should be encouraged to buy and use such vehicles. We must find alternatives to petroleum. Bio-fuels can be such alternatives.

3. People should be taught about how they can use fuel more efficiently. They must turn their vehicles off when they have to wait at a red signal for a couple of minutes or when they are stuck in a traffic jam.

4. We should try to explore and find more petroleum reserves in our own country.

Our suggestion: India can save a lot of money if it finds alternatives to oil and oil products. It will not only make us more independent, but will also help reduce air pollution, which is caused by the vehicles (Solar-powered vehicles and electric cars do not emit smoke).

67. Doctors' Work – Service or Business? (or Hospitals as Business Centres?)

As a service:

1. A doctor's work is sacred work. Doctors save thousands of lives everyday, and because of this, many people in India compare them with God. They should not degrade their position in the society by making this sacred work a business.

2. People trust doctors because they believe that their doctors will take the best possible decisions for their health (and not for own pockets). Doctors should not break the trust of their patients by keeping business above service. It is an ethical obligation of every doctor to keep the service first. When the medical profession becomes a business, service takes a back seat. Doctors start prescribing the medicine and tests that suit their own business needs rather than delivering the best possible treatments to the patients. Sometimes, they carry out unnecessary tests, or prescribe a number of medicines even if a patient doesn't need

them. Some doctors prescribe the expensive medicines even if the less expensive ones are available.

3. Malpractices in the medical profession are unforgivable because it directly affects the lives of people. When a service becomes a business, a room is created for malpractices including corruption. Some doctors have been found selling kidneys of their patients.

As a business:

1. Even doctors are human beings. When everyone else in the society is doing business, why should doctors not earn some extra bucks?
2. Private hospitals run by the money they earn from their patients, not by government aid. They are businesses and they need funds. The more money they make, the better services they can provide to the patients.
3. Malpractices happen in every profession. Moreover, only a few doctors are involved in malpractices. Why defame all the doctors for them?

Our suggestion: It is a ground reality that the medical profession is now a business as well a service; and there's nothing wrong with that unless the business aspect of this profession completely shadows the service aspect. If the doctors don't indulge in unethical practices, they have every right to make money. India's medical associations and the Indian government must take care that the health of the patients is not pushed to the second place in the chase for money. Doctors who are found guilty of being involved in unethical medical practices must be punished. Only then malpractices could be stopped.

68. Child Labour – Is It Wrong?

In favour of child labour:

Some families in India are so poor that the parents cannot even feed their children twice a day. In such families, every member, child or adult, has to work to earn bread. If the children won't work, they or their parents will have to sleep with empty stomach.

Against child labour:

1. Child labour is a cruel practice. Children are supposed to study and play. Childhood is the period when their physical and mental developments take place. If they are forced to work and earn a living, their overall development gets badly affected because they get no time for children's activities (exploring the world, learning about things, enjoying games, etc.).

2. By allotting their study time to work, children give up their hopes of a better future; and it happens when children are allowed to work because usually people do force them to work. In other words, child labour also leads to children's exploitation.

3. People opt for more number of children if the children are allowed to earn. People think that more children (especially boys, as they're considered comparatively stronger) will earn more money for family. This way, child labour adds to the problem of population explosion and female foeticide.

4. We have no right to take away a child's childhood from him. It is against humanity.

Our suggestion: Government and the society will have to come together to stop the menace of child labour. It is everyone's responsibility to make sure that children do not go to bed hungry; unless we ensure that the basic needs of a child are fulfilled, child labour will not stop. If children are working for food, if we can't provide them a free childhood they deserve, how can we call ourselves a civilized society? Child labour must stop. The child-protection NGOs can play a lead role in stopping child labour.

69. Effects of Cinema on Youth

Movies are meant for entertainment. No movie, even if based on a real-life story, can be 100% true (unless it is a documentary or specifically intended to show the truth) because the director has to sell the tickets, and for that he must add some entertainment to it. Movies take a young person in a world they can only dream about; a world full of excitement, action, valour and emotions. But drifting into an unreal world may have some effects on the conscious and subconscious minds of the people (you do get shivers when you watch a horror movie even if you don't want to).

Positive effects:

1. Most movies have a hero and a villain, and in the end part, the villain loses his life or reputation. This means that the movies are conveying the right message to the youth by showing the downfall of bad. In a way, they are motivating young people to lead a good life.

2. Movies based on patriotic stories and lives of great men encourage the young ones to do something worthwhile for the nation and the world.

3. Movies based on the historical events or epics acquaint our youth with the history and ancient culture of our nation. They help the youth understand their civilization better.

4. Movies based on social problems and issues motivate young people to act against the problems our society is facing. Movies based on dowry teach a young man why he should not accept dowry. Movies based on corruption educate the youth how corruption is eating up the very roots of our society.

5. Movies often display an ideal world; the world of dreams. When young people watch such movies, they are motivated to turn that ideal world into a reality.

6. Some movies inspire young people to do something great in life. For instance, a movie based on a great discovery can motivate young people to become scientists and discover something.

Movies based on sports motivate people to win medals for the nation.

7. Heroic deeds depicted in the movies give the youth courage to stare in the face of difficulties.

8. Movies often display the global cultures. They make people broad-minded by introducing different viewpoints and cultures to them. We learn a lot from the movies.

Negative effects:

1. Since the movies take people into an unreal world, the young ones often forget the realities of life and learn to live in a fantasy world. They spend more time watching movies and less time doing something worthwhile. In short, they learn to waste time on movies.

2. Movies are not all good. Some movies show how a bad person gets everything he wants using wrong means (even though he's punished in the end, he's got what he wanted in life!). Such movies may push young people towards crimes. (Many youngsters have been caught stealing vehicles to buy the things they want; something as unimportant as a new gadget or a bottle of wine!)

3. Glorification of violence is often seen in the movies. Actors settle their issues using muscle power rather than using legal ways. This motivates young people to take law into their own hands and fight others. Movies often show a hero fighting multiple villains bare handed or jumping from a tree or a terrace. If a young person tries to imitate such actions in a real-life situation, he may lose his life! Moreover, when a young man can't do what he has seen his favourite hero (who has been trained for years to perform an action) doing in a movie, he feels discouraged.

4. Some movies glorify drinking and smoking. They send a message that forming smoke rings or a hangover is cool. They promote these unhealthy habits.

5. Some movies picture young ones breaking the traffic rules, fooling the policemen and the society, living a careless life. When a person tries to do the same in real life, he may end up in a jail or a hospital.

6. Some movies have excessive sexual content, which may misguide the youth. It also goes against the Indian culture. India is a land where people used to compare women with great women like Queen Lakshmi Bai of Jhansi, Mother Teresa and Goddess Sita. Cheap movies encourage the youth to do the opposite. Consequently, now there are so many crimes (rapes, molestations, eve-teasing, etc.) against the women in our society. To an extent, these cheap movies are also responsible for these crimes.

7. Movies often push the society towards materialism. Rich characters in the movies often enjoy a dream life (while in real life, even the rich people face many problems). Such movies encourage the youth to participate in the blind race for money.

8. Some movies show the things which may be prevalent in some societies but may not be understood appropriate in others. When the directors directly borrow (or plagiarize) scenes and stories of foreign movies, they may unintentionally offend the local culture and values.

Our suggestion: Cinema has both positive and negative effects on the youth of a nation. Here two things should be kept in mind: Firstly, society (especially the parents) must make their children understand the difference between real world and fantasy world. If a young person takes movies only as entertainment, he will not be swayed away by what is shown in them. Secondly, it depends on the youth white kind of movies they prefer. A young person may choose to see the movies which inculcate good values and teach something worthwhile; alternatively, he may watch those movies, which provide cheap entertainment at the cost of time and values. But one should never forget that movies are just movies.

70. Capitalism, Communism and Socialism

Capitalism:

Capitalism is a political and economic system in which properties and means of production (factories, machines, etc.) may be (and usually are) owned by the individuals and organisations (Private ownership is a major characteristic of capitalism). In such a system, people and organisations can compete with each other for profits and can accumulate wealth too. Prices of goods and services are determined by the free market forces in capitalism. Government either has less or nominal control over prices.

Some of the economies which are considered to be capitalists are the USA, England, Canada, Australia, Japan, South Korea, Belgium, Netherlands, etc.

Advantages of Capitalism: Since people can compete for profits, they put more efforts in innovations and inventions. These innovations and inventions help the society to move ahead, technologically and otherwise. People get more choices in work and they are free to do more profiteering works. They get motivation and chance to get ahead in life; they put their heart into profit-making activities. People get wide range of products and services. Naturally, more jobs are created in such a system.

Disadvantages of Capitalism: People get divided in classes according to the amount of wealth they possess. People become greedy and some even indulge in unethical business practices to get rich. Rich people often get an edge over the others (in healthcare, decision making, quality of life and education, wherever money is required). The gap between the rich and the poor may go on increasing. Businesses can make monopoly-like situations sometimes.

Communism:

Communism is a political and economic system in which properties and means of production are owned by the governments of the communist countries, and emphasis is laid on equal distribution of wealth among the people. Government has either complete or almost complete control over the economy. In pure form of communism, each person works according to his capabilities and is paid according to his needs. The basic idea behind communism is equality among people. Principles of communism oppose accumulation of wealth by the individuals.

Some of the communist countries are China, Vietnam, Cuba, etc.

Advantages of Communism: People care more about each other because there's no competition for wealth accumulation. People can live with a peace of mind. All are considered (and are supposed to be) equal. People work according to their capabilities. People are not fired suddenly (as companies can't cut jobs to make profits). Monopoly cannot be created by companies (as the government controls everything).

Disadvantages of Communism: People do not get many choices in work. They have less personal freedom. They don't get special rewards even if they work with more dedication. All the power lies in the hands of the government, and when corruption seeps into the system, people are ruled by powerful and corrupt authorities. Innovation takes a backseat because in the absence of economic rewards, people don't get enough motivation.

Socialism:

Socialism lies somewhere between capitalism and communism. In a socialist system, means of production are owned by the society. The basic idea behind socialism is common ownership by the whole society. Every member of the society is given the right to participate in the decisions that affect everyone in the society. An emphasis is laid on the formation of cooperatives. Even the principles of socialism discourage accumulation of wealth by individuals.

You might have noticed that socialism and communism are similar in many respects. In fact, some people believe that communism is an extreme form of socialism.

Advantages and disadvantages of socialism: (Very much like advantages and disadvantages of communism.)

India is a socialist republic which is said to be headed towards capitalism, though it has not become a fully capitalistic economy yet (and it was never 100% socialist either).

To tell the truth, in the present world, no country may be full capitalist/communist/socialist, though any country may be bent towards one of these systems. The countries have mixed economic systems. Communist countries have billionaires and capitalist governments keep an eye on their companies and markets.

71. Linking of the Rivers in India

India is working on a National River Linking Project (NRLP). Our former president, Dr. A.P.J. Abdul Kalam has shown particular interest in this project, because it can solve many river-water related problems in India.

Advantages:

1. By linking two or more rivers through canals, we can make sure that water will reach those parts of the country which are relatively dry and face the problem of drought repeatedly. Irrigation will be possible in such areas (For example, the dry parts of Rajasthan and MP could be provided excess water through canals).

2. By linking the rivers, we can prevent floods. Water of those rivers which flow above the safe levels during rains could be diverted to other rivers which have no danger of flood. For example, Bihar has been cursed by floods in river Kosi. If the flood water could be diverted to other rivers, we would be able to save many lives. Mumbai floods could be prevented too.

3. Water could be distributed more evenly throughout the nation.

4. Canal water can be used to produce hydroelectric power.

Disadvantages:

1. At some places, people will have to be relocated to other areas (which happens whenever the water level changes in an area).

2. Some ecosystems will get badly affected.

3. Sometimes, the neighbouring countries object to such river-linking projects because diverting the water of a river may affect them too.

Our suggestion: The project of linking the rivers of India is a pain worth taking because it will provide permanent solution to the problem of floods and droughts in many parts of the country. It should be done, though carefully.

72. Pokhran Nuclear Tests – Have They Helped Us or Harmed Us?

India conducted five nuclear tests in May 1998 (popularly called Pokhran-II or Operation Shakti). Many experts and countries pointed finger at India's nuclear tests, saying that India has gained nothing by conducting these tests. But has India really gained anything except economic bans from these tests? Well, the answer is NO. Here's what India has gained by conducting the nuclear tests:

1. It had become very important for India to conduct the nuclear tests because India is surrounded by the neighbours (namely China and Pakistan) that have fought wars with India. It is a well-known fact that China has a large arsenal of nuclear weapons, and even Pakistan had been gaining nuclear power and technology before India's tests (or how could it have conducted nuclear tests right after India did?). Therefore, to maintain a balance of power with these countries, India needed to conduct the nuclear tests.

2. These tests have proved that India has nuclear capabilities and it can make nuclear weapons if needed. Since India has already stated that India's nuclear weapons are only for peaceful purpose and they will not be used first against any country, nobody needs to fear India's nuclear program. Moreover, the nuclear weapons act as a deterrent against any nuclear aggression from an enemy. This way they help maintain peace in a region.

3. Conducting nuclear tests is an accomplishment of Indian science. These tests are not conducted only for the purpose of making weapons, but they also provide important data about other uses of nuclear power (such as nuclear energy).

4. Power respects power. Even if a nation doesn't want nuclear weapons, it is strategically advantageous to prove own nuclear capabilities. By conducting the nuclear tests, India joined the elite nuclear club. It became a regional power and increased its chances of gaining a permanent seat in the United Nations Security Council. Had India not conducted the nuclear tests, could it have proved that it was a responsible nuclear power? No.

5. Since a responsible nuclear state is respected globally, it also attracts business from other countries. Therefore, these tests will prove to be economically advantageous for the nation in the long run.

Our suggestion: The Pokhran nuclear tests have helped India establish itself as a regional power and they will prove to be vital for the future of the country.

73. Honour Killing

In layman's terms, honour killing can be described as killing a person (or more than one person) for the sake of honour, because the people who kill believe that the victim had brought dishonour upon a family/group/community/society/race through his or her actions. Honour killing is not a new phenomenon; the history of many countries is full of examples of honour killing. Though even in the present time such incidences happen in many countries (such as India, Pakistan, countries of the Middle East, Italy, Bangladesh, etc.), we will be focussing on honour killing in India (because that's what you're likely to be asked in a GD).

Honour Killing in India:

Cases of honour killing have been reported from many states of India. The reasons which are given for these killings are as follows:

1. A girl wanted to marry (or married) against her parents' wish or community's rules
2. A person wanted to marry outside his caste (inter-caste marriage) or inside his own *'goutra'*.
3. People doubted the character of a person.
4. A specific action of a married person (it may be sexual or otherwise) brought dishonour to his family or the entire community.
5. Pre-marital or extramarital love affairs.
6. Deceiving own husband/wife for another person.

Are honour killings justified? The answer is 'no'. No one in the society has a right to take law into one's own hands. The Indian constitution doesn't permit that.

What can be done to stop Honour Killings:

1. Since honour killing is a social problem, the first step that must be taken is to make people understand that they should not (and cannot) take law into their own hands, because doing so makes them criminals in the eyes of law and they will be punished for their crime.
2. People must not make their children marry against their wishes because if a marriage takes place against one of the partners' wishes, there are high chances of failure of such marriage.

3. People must understand that no court is above the court of law. The Indian law is applicable on every Indian citizen and community.

4. People must understand that no religion allows a person to kill another person. Every religion condemns the killings of innocent people.

5. We should have strict laws (and properly implement those laws) to stop honour killings.

Our suggestion: Honour killings also malign the image of a society and a country. When people in other countries come to know about such incidences, they wonder about the law and order situation of that nation. Honour killings must be stopped.

74. Is Sex Education Important?

Sex education is the education about various aspects of sexual behaviour. These aspects are reproduction, sexual intercourse, birth control, sex-related crimes, and anatomy of sex organs. Many countries provide sex education to the students in schools, while some countries believe it is not appropriate to do so. Some countries have just not started it yet.

We believe that sex education should be a part of education of a person (though at what age a student can benefit most from sex education is something that the authorities need to decide), because providing sex education has many benefits for the society. These benefits are like this:

1. Sex education can help in preventing devastating diseases like AIDS. If a person has been provided sex education, he is less likely to fall in unsafe sexual relations. So, sex education can work as a weapon against AIDS and other sexually transmittable diseases.

2. Sex education will help prevent the cases of sexual exploitation of children and women. An aware person will not fall victim to sexual crimes because he will have knowledge about his rights.

3. Providing sex education may help our nation control the rapidly growing population, as the subject of 'birth control' also comes under sex education.

4. Understanding anatomy of organs is good for a person's health. It may help prevent, recognise and cure many diseases.

5. Sex education may answer the questions a person wants to ask but doesn't ask because of shyness.

75. Cloning – Is It Ethical?

Science has made so much advancement that now the scientists can prepare clone of a living organism by using its DNA. It must be noted that a clone doesn't mean exactly the same-looking individual (as is usually shown in the movies), but an individual with identical genetic properties. Clone is sometimes called 'baby with identical genes'.

Cloning is a giant leap in the field of medical sciences, and some people believe it will help the human kind lead a better life, while others believe that cloning is unethical and it interferes with God's and nature's work. Here are some of the advantages and disadvantages of cloning:

Advantages of cloning:

1. Cloning can help the sterile people have children. The parents who cannot otherwise reproduce, can provide their DNA, and with the help of this DNA, the scientists can produce genetically similar babies.

2. Cloning can also help in regenerating the cells damaged by a disease or an accident. Thus, a non-functioning organ may be turned into a functioning one by replacing its dead cells with new ones. It may greatly help in the recovery treatment of lethal diseases like stroke, heart-attack, cancer, etc. It may also help prevent the diseases like diabetes and hypertension that run in the families.

3. A clone may donate organs to the DNA-donor individual. For instance, a clone's kidneys, lungs and heart could be perfect match for the donor individual needing them. Moreover, the transplants could be done without the fear of new organs being rejected by the recipient's body. (But this point is debatable because some people don't think it appropriate to create clones just for the benefit of a person. They say that the clones should not be treated as second-grade individuals whose organs can be donated to others.)

4. Talks are also going on about whether cloning can provide consumable meat, so it will reduce the number of animals being killed for meat every year.

Disadvantages of cloning:

1. Some people believe that the cloned individuals will be treated as second-class organisms created to fulfil the specific objectives (objectives such as donating organs, or performing well in particular fields, such as sports, etc.).

2. Some people fear that the cloned individuals the will be exactly like the original individuals and there'll be a conflict of identities (a misapprehension created by movies), or may be the clones of bad people will be created. (But it's not true because the environment plays a significant role in shaping the behaviour of an individual. The clone of a cruel person, if brought up in a kind environment, could be a kind person!)

3. Some scientists believe that by producing the cloned individuals, we can lose precious 'genetic variation', which helps the species survive in the long run (by bringing genetic modifications, which adapt an organism to survive the phenomenon of 'natural selection'.)

4. Some religious people believe that we must not interfere with nature's (or God's) job by creating replicas of individuals.

Our suggestion: Cloning can open the new doors in the field of medical sciences. It can save thousands of lives and give new hopes to the handicapped people. The only hurdle is, once again, human greed. We can misuse the power of cloning (just like any other power) or we can use it for the service of humanity.

76. Should Large States be Divided into Smaller Ones?

Many large states of India have been divided into smaller ones. MP was divided into MP and Chhattisgarh, Bihar into Bihar and Jharkhand, UP into UP and Uttarakhand, Punjab into Punjab and Haryana, and so on. Many people have advocated the formation of separate states of Vidarbha and Telangana. The real question is whether it is favourable for the nation to create smaller states by dividing the larger ones. Here are some of the advantages and disadvantages of creating the smaller states:

Advantages of creating smaller states:

1. It is believed that in small states, development is more even. For instance, a large state has a few big cities and many smaller ones; and usually the emphasis is laid on developing big cities and less attention is paid to the smaller cities. Most of the investment is directed towards big cities only. But when a large state is divided, some of its smaller cities become major cities of the newly formed states (because each small state has less number of cities). Then it becomes easy to develop the previously neglected cities. (Many people in the large states complain that their city is not developing as rapidly because a metro is drawing all the attention.)

2. The smaller states are easier to govern. A Chief Minister can take better care of a smaller area than a big area. It becomes easy to keep an eye on the law and order in a smaller area with less population.

3. The creation of small states may help fight corruption. The already established nexus between the corrupt people will break because the natural resources (and their control) will be divided between two states.

4. The large states have a lot of diversity in themselves. For example, in a single large state, some communities live in the hilly areas, others in the plains, and still others near the sea. The people living in the hills may complain that their government knows very little about their problems and it focuses more on the larger population living in the plains or near the sea, so they must have a separate government which can understand them better. In the smaller states, there are few such problems because they have less diversity.

Disadvantages of creating smaller states:

1. If the states are divided in the name of religions and communities, it would be a disaster for the unity of our nation, because people of such states will be even more intolerant towards each other.

2. Sometimes, people demand the division of a state because a selfish politician is encouraging them to do so for his own gains. If the states are formed on such basis, it can't be good for the nation.

3. Managing large number of states can be a tough job for the central government of India.

4. If the basis of division is language and culture, then regionalism will prosper in the country and the unity will be put into danger.

Our suggestion: If the states are divided, it should not be in the name of religion, language, culture or region, but only for the development of every part of the nation. Division must also not be for anyone's personal gains, but for the right reasons.

77. Money is Needed to Make Money (or Money Begets Money)

In favour:

1. People who have money, invest it in the real estate, stock market and elsewhere to multiply their wealth. Therefore, it is true that money begets money.
2. People who have large amounts of money, do not need to look at others for investing in their projects. They can use their own money in their money-making projects.
3. Rich people join other rich people's society where they get more ideas to make money. Using those ideas they make even more money.
4. Even if money is kept in the bank accounts, it accumulates interest. The bigger the amount deposited, the more the amount of interest on it. Therefore, money makes more money.

Against:

1. No doubt that money can be used to make more money, but there also have been the people who started with a scratch and made unparallel business empires. Warren Buffet, Bill Gates, Dhirubhai Ambani, N.R. Narayana Murthy and many other business tycoons began with very little amount and became billionaires. This proves that to make money, we need wisdom, courage, knowledge, dedication, perseverance and ideas, not just money. Even those who begin with paltry amounts, can make huge amounts of money.
2. If a person has a great idea and sufficient knowledge, he can convince the rich people to invest in his idea. That's how many big firms were started (with the investments from angel investors – the people who invest in others' ideas and projects). Therefore, even without money, a person can make money.

3. There have been the authors who became rich by writing the bestselling books; there have been the motivational speakers who only had the gift of the gab (gift of being able to speak well); there have been the athletes who make lots of money because of their athletic skills.

4. Then obviously there are the exceptionally lucky people who buy a lottery ticket and win a jackpot! What is their initial investment? Almost nothing. All they need is luck! *(Note: This is a weak point.)*

Our suggestion: Money can be used to make more money, but not always does a person need money to make money. The talented people usually find ways of making money, even if they have too little or nothing to begin with. However, you can't completely disagree that money begets money.

78. Linking Religion and Politics – Is It Okay?

There has not been a single nation in the world where religion has not had any impact on the politics and vice-versa. However, when we talk about India, religion and politics greatly affect each other. Sometimes, the politicians draw the principles of politics from the religions, and sometimes, the religious gurus become politicians (or affect the results of elections). Sometimes, the fates of the candidates are decided by their religion, and sometimes, religious clashes take place with the support of the politicians. Let's evaluate the pros and cons of linking religion and politics in India:

Pros:

1. Politics can learn a lot from religion. Religion has always helped a person understand the difference between good and bad, right and wrong. Religion has the element of ancient wisdom in it. Based on what they have learned from religion, the politicians can choose the right course of action for the nation. Religion can suggest the right path to the politicians. Similarly, people can use the wisdom of religion to choose the right person for this duty.

2. Even the presidents and prime ministers of many countries take a religious oath to serve their nations to the best of their abilities. Religion provides a reason for a person to be good.

3. Many people, including many politicians and voters, fear the religious consequences of the bad deeds. This way religion keeps them away from the bad actions.

Cons:

1. If religion becomes the basis of choosing a candidate, people give priority to a less worthy candidate of their religion over a worthier candidate of some other religion. This way religion becomes a barrier between country and its progress.

2. Many politicians use religious feelings of the people to spread hatred and secure own vote banks. They, sometimes, even organise communal riots in which hundreds of innocent people are killed.

3. Sometimes, people vote for the candidate, who was endorsed by a particular religious guru. Such candidate may be a puppet in the hands of that guru, and may not be able to do any good to the nation.

4. In many nations, where religion is above everything else (including politics), anything that is against any aspect of religion, becomes unacceptable; no matter how essential it is for the welfare of that nation. The politicians cannot act with an open mind. Such countries would be too lucky if they still manage to develop, because certain aspects of religions get old as the time passes.

Our suggestion: Religion and politics will continue to affect each other to an extent, but when the limit is crossed, it becomes not only bad but sometimes dangerous for the future of the country. Keeping the mentioned points in mind, it can be said that religion and politics must maintain their individual identities and they should not overpower each other in a democracy.

79. Food Adulteration in India

When a cheaper and inferior substance is added to a food item to increase its quantity artificially, it is called food adulteration. Some examples of food adulteration are – mixing urea and water in milk, mixing stones in foodgrains, mixing dyes in edible colours, etc. The main objective of food adulteration is to make more profits by selling artificially increased quantities of food items. Of course, it is an illegal and unethical practice.

How food adulteration harms us:

1. Adulterants are often harmful to human health. Sometimes, they are poisonous too! Consuming an adulterated food item can even cause food poisoning. Hundreds of people have died after drinking adulterated wine. Thousands of children get ill after drinking milk adulterated with unclean water. Food adulteration may cause multiple diseases such as diarrhoea, infections of the respiratory tract, fever, vomiting, indigestion and other abdominal diseases, etc. Children are at a greater danger because their immune systems are not as strong as those of adults. It is a bitter truth that people endanger others' lives for their own profits.

2. Food adulteration financially harms the consumers. A person pays full price for a food item and he gets less than the promised quantity of it. For instance, you pay for pulses and you get a cheap mixture of pulses and stones! It's a loss.

3. Food adulteration may not show its adverse effects immediately, but it may affect the health of people in the long run. Physical and mental development of people may get affected if they consume adulterated items for a long time. In other words, it acts as slow poison.

4. Food adulteration gives rise to more corruption in the society, because in order to keep the authorities and other people quiet, the adulterator might pay bribes to them.

Our suggestion: Food adulteration is nothing less than a heinous crime against the society. It directly affects the health of the people. Incidences of adulteration must be reported to the authorities immediately and the adulterators should be put behind the bars. There must be stricter laws against food adulteration. The consumer may also go to the consumer court to get justice. It is the need of the hour to free our society from this malpractice.

80. Vision-2020 for India

Vision-2020 is the name given to a program envisioned by Dr. A.P.J. Abdul Kalam to turn India into a developed nation by 2020. The program sets the goals in five domains:

Infrastructure and electricity: Interlinking of rivers, creating urban amenities in the rural areas, and solar farming, etc.

Agriculture: To ensure the food security of the Indians by doubling the production of food.

Education and healthcare: To create better healthcare facilities for all and to end illiteracy.

IT and communication: To maintain India's dominance in the field of Information Technology and utilize IT in various fields like healthcare, communication, education, etc.

Critical technology and industry: Development of nuclear and space technologies and defence related technologies.

Goals have been set to develop India in these five areas. These goals have been set by the experts in their respective fields. It is expected that even if all the goals are not reached by 2020, at least they will act as the guidelines for the future development of India. However, these goals are fully realistic and not mere dreams.

Benefits of Vision-2020:

1. Encouraged by Vision-2020, many experts in the different fields have set goals for progress. These goals will help India move ahead at a faster pace.

2. Vision-2020 has become so popular that not only the students but even the common man is talking about it. An awareness has been created that will help India in the future. An idea is now there and it will lead to action.

3. India has made nice progress in the last few years. Our economic data is indicative of this. Vision-2020 has definitely been a motivation behind it.

Some people argue that India has a lot of problems, such as large population, corruption, illiteracy, etc., so it cannot become a developed nation by 2020. However, as mentioned earlier, Vision-2020 is not a set of stringent goals which, if not fulfilled by 2020, would fail; it's a set of realistic goals that, even if not fulfilled by the set time, will help the nation move ahead on the path of development. The Indians must make Vision-2020 their own vision.

81. Mass Migration Towards the Metros in India

It is a well-known fact that people from the rural areas and smaller cities have been moving into the metro cities for various reasons. Some of the major reasons behind this migration are:

1. One can easily find a job in or near a metro city. There are ample jobs available for both the skilled and unskilled people in a metro, because both the national and multinational companies (MNCs) tend to set up their operations either in a metro city or an industrial area near it. The jobs are not that easy to find in small cities and villages.

2. The basic amenities such as schools, colleges, hospitals, etc. are available in the metros. Moreover, the metros have more reputed educational institutions and health facilities. That's why people want to live in or near a metro in the hope of a better life. The reputed University of Delhi attracts hundreds of students every year and thousands of patients from all over the country come and get treated in the AIIMS.

3. In the metro cities, more opportunities of getting rich are available. Moreover, large customer base is what a businessman wants. The more the number of people, the more the customers for every business. A shopkeeper can sell larger quantities of products in the metros. A rickshaw-puller, who makes Rs. 100 daily in a small city, can make Rs. 200 or more in a metro on daily basis.

4. More choices are available in a metro city. More brands of clothes, more types of restaurants, more number of markets, more kinds of courses for the students, and what not.

5. There are the villages that hardly get electricity a couple of hours daily. Some villages don't have roads; some don't have high schools, colleges, railway lines or hospitals. When the people living in such areas look for the alternative places to live, the metros seem attractive to them.

6. Reputation is another factor. Those who live in the metros are understood to be living in modern societies in which people can live the way they want to; they can wear what they want, eat what they like and act as they want. People want to be a part of these modern societies, so they come and settle in the metros.

When mass migration occurs towards a particular area, it suffers a lot because its limited resources get divided between huge number of people. Result: Scarcity of water, traffic jams on roads, no beds in hospitals, no seats in schools and colleges, tightly packed city buses, hard-to-find residences, high rents of rooms, queues for everything, etc.

How to stop mass migration towards the metros:

1. Government should create the basic amenities like hospitals, schools, etc. in villages and towns.

2. Electricity should reach every village. Each village should be connected to the cities by the network of roads and railways.

3. Companies should be offered tax concessions if they create jobs in the rural and semi-urban areas.

4. People should be told about the benefits of living in villages and small cities. Some of the benefits are fresh, unpolluted air to breathe, organic crops to eat, no traffic jams, no congested areas, less expensive services, etc.

Our suggestion: In short, we can say that if the development in all parts of the nation is even, people will have more choices of places to live in. Unless there are sufficient facilities available in the small cities, towns and villages, mass migration towards the metros will continue to take place.

82. Criminalisation of Politics

The Parliaments and legislative assemblies are understood to be the temples of democracy in India. People look at them with the hope that the elected people sitting in these temples will provide them a clean governance and justice. But when people with a tainted history are elected, a common man is compelled to rethink whether he can expect a clean rule and justice from them. It has happened once and again that the candidates charged with heinous crimes such as murder, ballet-booth capturing, riots, etc. were elected. In 2002, the Supreme Court of India made it compulsory for the candidates to declare their criminal records along with their educational qualifications and finances. Though it has proved to be a very important step to educate people about the candidates, it has not been one-hundred percent successful in preventing the criminals from entering the politics and ruling the people.

In a democracy (such as ours), power lies in the hands of the chosen representatives. When the criminals get this power, they may try to get cleared of the charges made against them by threatening the policemen and judges, they may try to maintain their reign by threatening people and capturing ballet-booths during the elections, they may try to make money through the criminal activities, and they may even organise riots. If many people with criminal record enter the politics, it also maligns the image of the nation in the International community.

How do the criminals make it to the Parliament and legislative assemblies? May be in some cases, by capturing the polling-booths or changing the ballet boxes, but in most cases, people choose them. Either people may not have the knowledge of a candidate's criminal record, or they may be threatened and forced to vote for that person, or may be people choose them for petty reasons such as he belongs to their caste or religion, etc. It also happens sometimes that people have no choice but to choose one between two or more criminal candidates contesting an election. It is highly unlikely that people vote for a person with tainted record because they believe such person has reformed and he's worthier than any candidate with a clean record.

How can people prevent the criminalisation of politics? By voting for the right candidate who has a clean record, and by refusing to vote under any pressure or sell their votes. It is also important that people who truly think about the welfare of the society come forward and contest the elections. Suggestion of providing a 'No Vote' or 'Right to reject' option to voters in all elections has also been made by various NGOs, politicians and social workers from time to time. According to this option, voters will have a right to 'not vote' for any candidate contesting the election if they don't find one with a clean record, and then the election will be held again with fresh faces. Awareness must be created among people so that they don't vote for a candidate without knowing his history.

Our suggestion: It is very unfortunate for a nation to be ruled by the people with criminal records. It is the duty of every citizen to vote for the right candidate and keep the criminals away from politics. Representatives of the people should be those who anyone can trust. Vote is the ultimate power in people's hand and they must use it wisely.

83. Group Discussion

(Note: Don't get surprised if you get the topic 'Group Discussion' to discuss. It's not an uncommon topic.)

In layman's language, when more than two people come together and discuss a mutually agreed topic to reach a consensus (or to find solution to the problem discussed), the process is called group discussion. But for a student, group discussion can be more than just a discussion, because it can be a part of the selection process of a reputed institute or company. For an MBA aspirant, group discussion is something important to master.

What is the need of a GD?

A group discussion is a method to find solution to a given problem. When many minds come together to discuss an issue, it becomes more probable to find a solution or reach a consensus (or, at least, a rational decision). It helps to see an issue from different peoples' viewpoints.

An organisation conducts group discussion because before it recruits a candidate, it wants to make sure that the candidate is suitable for that particular job. For instance, if it's a sales job, the candidate must have a right mix of assertiveness and willingness to serve so that he or she can sell the product and retain the customers. If it's an administration related position, the candidate must be able to display confidence in front of others. A B-School organises a group discussion to select the candidates with managerial traits. These traits can be easily spotted during a professional group discussion, as there is time pressure in addition to the pressure to perform. Moreover, an evaluator would be able to see the true colours of a person during the tense conditions of group discussion, because people often reflect their hidden traits when they are busy discussing with multiple people.

How one can succeed in a group discussion:

A person can succeed in a group discussion by displaying the skills required for the post (or seat) he is applying for. For instance, if you display the managerial skills (such as leadership qualities, patience, effective communication skills, team spirit, confidence, etc.), you have better chances to get selected for a managerial position or a B-School seat. A sales aspirant may display how he can be assertive without being too pushy to sell a product; a finance person can display he can use financial language while talking to a customer; an HR aspirant can display he can get the work done by managing the people effectively. (However, it is unwise to try to fake the qualities one doesn't have. Instead one should develop those qualities by watching or reading about the leaders in those respective fields. For instance, news anchors can teach a lot about communication skills and great leaders can teach a lot about the leadership qualities.). Also, a person gets an opportunity to display his knowledge in a group discussion. A person who reads newspaper columns and magazines regularly will certainly be able to add latest information to the discussion. So, a person needs to add to his pool of knowledge continuously in order to succeed in a group discussion.

How to make a discussion successful:

The members of a group must act sensibly to make a discussion successful. They must forget their mutual conflicts and focus on the issue in hand. They must put their genuine viewpoints forward and provide relevant examples to make others understand those viewpoints. They must not waste time in discussing irrelevant or less relevant matters, and they must seek clarification from others if they don't understand something.

(You can also discuss the myths about group discussion, and how it feels to be amidst a discussion.)

84. Education – A Business?

Education is something no society can take lightly. Quality of the education provided directly affects the personalities and characters of the people of the society. It also determines how successful a person will be in his field and what field is good for a person. In ancient India, education was provided through a tradition commonly known as *'guru-shishya parampara'* (a sacred tradition in which a guru imparts education to his students), but over the last few years, this face of education has changed dramatically. Schools have been turned into businesses and anyone willing to make a good fortune sees starting a school as a viable option (regardless of whether he is qualified for the responsibility or not). Not only hefty tuition fees and bus fares are charged from the parents but they are also asked for heavy donations in the name of the development of schools. So is true about colleges. Business schools charge lakhs of rupees from every student and they also make money by selling prospectuses of their programs. This phenomenon has given rise to the question whether education should be just a business or something more than that?

Pros of turning educational institutions into businesses:

1. If educational institutes make money, they can provide world class facilities to their students. Better libraries, better labs, more computers, more comfortable classrooms and buses, better sports equipment, bigger playgrounds, and what not! It's all good for the students. Moreover, creating more facilities will attract students from other countries as well. This will make our schools and colleges truly international level institutes.

2. If the educational institutes charge more, they can recruit better teachers and coaches, who demand high salaries. Thus, they'll be able to provide a better quality education to the students.

3. Some B-Schools, schools and colleges also have 'student exchange' tie ups with institutes of other countries. Such ties help

the students and teachers learn from their global counterparts. It will only be possible if the Indian institutions have high quality infrastructure and facilities.

4. Some educational institutions are associated with NGOs that work for the underprivileged children. They spend the excess money collected for the welfare of these children and the society.

Cons of turning educational institutions into businesses:

1. Education (especially the high quality education) will become unaffordable for the middle class and the poor people. Many parents still make a lot of compromises with their own dreams to send their children school because the fees are so high!

2. Many schools charge fees much higher than they should; and they often do so not for creating better facilities for children, but just for the sake of making money.

3. If the teachers only focus on making big money, they will not pay enough attention on how much the students are actually learning. All they will care about is keeping the job until someone else offers them higher salaries.

4. Some public schools, which often charge high fees, argue that their students get a better education than those studying in government institutions. However, the board exams results do not suggest so. Many times the students studying in the government schools (which have comparatively very low fees) make it to the top of the merit lists.

5. If the educational institutes become businesses, the families of the students will become customers who buy quality education for their children, and the teachers will become employees of a business. How can a customer respect a service provider as much as a student (and his family) respects a teacher? Education must not lose its higher position by turning into a business.

Our suggestion: In order to gain all the knowledge that a teacher has, a student needs to show due respect to him/her. If the teacher-student relation becomes a business-customer relation, teachers won't be interested in teaching the students all they can. We should maintain the reputation of a teacher's post by not turning education into a business. However, at the same time, we will have to accept the fact that in the changing times, the schools will need more money to operate better, and parents will have to bear with the increased school fees. There's nothing wrong with doing business, but at the same time, the schools must uphold our traditional values by keeping education a sacred tradition.

85. God Particle 'Higgs-Boson' – Does It Explain God?

Higgs-Boson, commonly called 'the God Particle', is a micro particle that has been found by the scientists during the world's largest experiment being done near Geneva (Switzerland), using the colossal machine 'Large Hadron Collider'. Many scientists believe that it is the very particle of which the whole universe is made up of and which is responsible for the weight of everything. Higgs Boson is named for Peter-Higgs, a notable scientist (Boson particle has been named after two great scientists – Satyendra Nath Bose and Albert Einstein). The discovery of Higgs Boson particle has been said to be one of the greatest discoveries of the century. This discovery will help the scientists understand our universe better.

Does Higgs Boson, the God particle, actually explain God? Many people won't agree. The discovery of Higgs-Boson is quite recent and science will have to go a long, long way to fully understand it. Only after understanding it, we will be able to tell whether this particle actually deserves to be called God particle. (Earlier, an expert had called it Goddamn particle because it wasn't being located despite the collective efforts of the scientists!) Therefore, before we fully understand something, it could be too early to say that it explains God (which, according to the religions, is the supreme power behind every creation, and cannot be defined fully). Nevertheless, like every major scientific discovery, this discovery too will help us understand our universe better. Therefore, we can say that whether this particle can explain God or not, this discovery takes us a step closer to understanding God.

86. India's Economic Growth

India has been one of the fastest growing major economies of the world in the past few years. The country that was compelled to mortgage its gold to other nations in the late 80s has touched the mark of 9% annual economic growth in the recent years. Even when the economic growth rate of many developed nations is either slightly above zero or in negative numbers, India has been able to maintain an appreciable growth rate. In 1991, India started with the policy of disinvestment, and since then the country has not looked back. In the recent years, the Indian companies have been able to buy some of the reputed foreign companies, and the Indians' purchasing power has increased too.

Some of the factors behind India's growth have been:

1. The story of India's economic growth began in 1991 when India opened its doors to the foreign investments (something China had done around a decade before India did). The public sector companies were made private and steps were taken to encourage foreign companies to come to India and create jobs. Disinvestment also boosted India's trade with other countries.

2. India is a favourite destination for the global investors. Many countries, including the UK, Mauritius, Singapore and the US have made direct investments (FDI) in India. One reason behind it is growing purchasing power of the people of India, which is attracting the investors. Also, India has a large pool of English speaking people, who work at salaries lesser than those of their Western counterparts, so many MNCs have set up their

BPOs here or outsourced IT work to the Indian companies. In addition, India has large number of skilled and unskilled labour and a trustable banking system. This makes India a lucrative destination for investment.

3. India has a large middle class. Such a huge consumer base is also a reason for economic growth of India. Growing domestic demand has helped India a lot. (This is also a reason why India is less likely to get affected by global economic fluctuations.)

4. The Indian household savings have also been a major contributor to the economic growth.

What can be done to further boost up the economic growth:

1. India will have to reduce the corruption, which is repulsing much more investment looking forward to come to the nation.

2. India must shorten the cumbersome processes of providing multiple licenses for setting up a business in the country. It will encourage the foreign businessmen to set up businesses in India.

3. India still needs to work on its infrastructure. If we create better roads, provide 24-hour electricity, improve communication system and provide better security, it will create trust among the international investor community.

4. We still need to go ahead with our disinvestment policy, though we cannot do it carelessly.

Our suggestion: India is doing well economically but can do even better if we take some positive steps. Since the tide of economic development seems to be in our favour at present, we must welcome it with open hands.

87. Inflation in India

A general increase in the prices of goods and services is termed inflation. It means that the purchasing power of the money you have keeps reducing as the inflation levels go up. For instance, if you were buying 5 kg of any vegetable for Rs 100 a year ago, now you'll get less of it for the same amount because inflation has reduced rupee's purchasing power. In India, inflation, which had recently touched the mark of 12%, has become a real headache; especially for the poor and middle-class people. The prices of things of daily needs, such as fruits and vegetables, milk, cereals, petrol and diesel, etc. touch the sky from time to time, and the budget of a common man topples. Let's understand what the causes of inflation are.

Causes of inflation:

1. When the value of the rupee goes down against the US dollar, it becomes expensive for the nation to import products from other countries. The country has to pay more money to buy the essential products like oil and gas, or to import food items from other countries (especially when the crops have been affected badly by weather). Therefore, the falling value of currency is a cause of inflation.

2. Any increase in the oil prices in the global market causes a proportional increase in the oil prices in our country. When the oil prices go up, the prices of almost everything shoot up because transportation costs increase. This is another cause of inflation in India.

3. India has a very large population, and it is growing fast. The demands of ever-growing population keep on increasing all the time and everything becomes scarce in the span of time. When the supply of goods is lower than the demand of goods, it leads to inflation.

4. Black marketing and hoarding of goods is another cause of inflation. Some greedy businessmen keep the goods stored (illegally) until there's a scarcity of those goods in the market. Then they sell the same goods at higher prices and make more profits. This is how inflation is created artificially.

5. When people earn more, their purchasing power increases and they buy more goods. This increased demand of goods exceeds the supply of goods in the market, and this leads to inflation.
6. There are some years not-so-good for agriculture. Either the monsoon comes late or it brings too little rains with it. The farmers cannot grow adequate crops to meet the demands of the country and this leads to inflation of the food products.
7. Corruption and black money are also the contributors to inflation. When people spend black money, it increases the demand of goods and services and they become scarce. This leads to high prices.
8. Sometimes, in order to counter recession, the central bank of the nation (RBI in India) prints more money. When the supply of goods is not in proportion to the money printed, the inflation goes up.
9. High taxes on the imported goods also lead to inflation.
10. When a country exports more of a product (despite its high demand in the country itself) in order to earn foreign currency, the product may become scarce in the domestic market and its prices shoot up.

Since inflation directly affects the lives of the people and also negatively impacts the economic growth of the nation, it needs to be countered.

How to fight inflation:

1. Government may reduce the taxes on imported essential commodities such as food products and oil. This helps bring down the inflation instantly.
2. Sometimes, the government imposes a ban on the export of certain products which are scarce in the domestic market. This helps lower the prices of those products because their supply in the domestic market increases.

3. The central bank (RBI) may increase the interest rates and control the liquidity in the market (and they do it from time to time). This helps reduce the inflation.

4. If our agriculture depends less on the rains, it would be good for the nation. Steps must be taken to ensure the uninterrupted supply of irrigation water to farms. Linking of major rivers may help in this.

5. Tough action must be taken against the hoarders and black marketers. Hoarding of essential commodities such as food products must not be allowed.

6. Steps should be taken to curb black money in the economy.

7. We need to take concrete measures to keep our population, which is already above a billion, under control.

Our suggestion: Inflation occurs in every nation, but, by taking certain appropriate measures, some nations have been able to keep it low. By taking the above-mentioned steps, we can control the inflation.

88. Should All the Public Sector Undertakings (PSUs) be Privatised?

Privatisation means turning the public sector organisations (or government organisations) into private organisations by selling their majority shares. (Some of the public sector companies in India are BHEL, ONGC, Power Grid, Indian Oil Corp., LIC, Air India, etc., and some of the private sector companies are Reliance Industries Ltd. (RIL), Infosys, HCL Tech, Tata Motors, Bajaj Auto Ltd. etc.)

In favour of privatisation:

1. In private organisations, the level of services and dedication of employees is usually high because the private owners expect high profits from the companies they own. Since they demand better results, employees need to put their best efforts in the work, and they do everything possible to keep the customers satisfied.

2. Employees in the private organisations also work better because they know that if they don't do so, their job may be given to someone else. In India, public sector jobs are considered as secure jobs, and, therefore, some employees take them lightly (as they know they'll not be fired).

3. Private organisations, in pursuit of more and more profits, tend to utilise the available resources more efficiently. This means that they produce more using less of the resources. One reason is that they cannot afford to waste resources (while the government organisations, having the government backing, do not focus that much on the efficiency).

4. By selling its stake in the public sector companies, the government earns a lot of money. This money can be used for various developmental activities (improvement of infrastructure, creating healthcare facilities, opening schools, etc.) or can be used for foreign exchange.

5. Red-tape creates room for more corruption in the public sector companies. Private sector has less of this problem.

6. Mismanagement is a major problem in the government undertakings. For instance, millions of tonnes of foodgrains are spoiled every year because we have a storage problem. Such things are less expected to happen in the private sector.

Disadvantages of privatisation:

1. What is the main purpose of having the public sector? Because people feel that certain things should remain in the hands of their trusted government, and they should be available to all the people. For instance, nation's security, drinking water, post offices, public hospitals, etc. People believe that they cannot handover such sensitive departments to someone whose ultimate goal is profit (and who might push public interest to the second place). Reliability is a major consideration in such domains (Nobody would want the security of the nation to be

compromised). Therefore, some public sector undertakings cannot be privatised.

2. Government has huge funds, and it can financially back some of its undertakings (banks, insurance companies, etc.). For instance, there are hardly any chances that a public sector bank will declare bankruptcy (that's why, many people keep their money in the government banks) or the government's insurance companies will not have sufficient funds to pay insurances. Such guarantees are barely available in the private sector companies.
3. Some sectors, such as nuclear energy, are simply too sensitive to be privatised.
4. Private sector is only interested in the areas where profit is there. Nobody wants to buy the ailing companies. Only the government takes care of such companies.
5. If all the government undertakings are privatised, many rural areas can get into a disadvantageous position because they do not generate high profits and the private organisations may not be interested in doing business in such areas.

Our suggestion: It may be the need of the hour to privatise some of the PSUs, but privatising all of them may not be a wise decision to take. Certain essential things are above profits, and the welfare of people should occupy first place in such areas.

89. Disaster Management in India

Disaster management is a crucial discipline that deals with the natural disasters (caused by earthquakes, floods, tsunamis, etc.) or man-made disasters (nuclear accidents, major gas leaks, explosions, etc.). Disasters can occur anywhere, anytime; a nation needs to always stay ready with pre- and post-disaster measures so that the loss of lives and capital can be minimised. In fact, with an effective disaster management system, we could have saved thousands of lives and billions of dollars that were lost due to the Gujarat and Maharashtra earthquakes, Assam and Bihar floods and Mumbai and Delhi bomb blasts. In India, National Disaster Management Authority (NDMA) is the apex body of disaster management.

Disaster management in India has been criticised on various grounds (people allege that they are not proactive, they often reach late, they do not have sufficient equipment, etc.).

The steps we need to take to prepare a better disaster management system are:

1. People should be trained about what they must do if any disaster takes place. (For instance, in case of an earthquake, they must get out of their houses and gather in open spaces, and they must not use a lift if the building is on fire.) By learning to act sensibly, people can survive a disaster and also save others' lives. Disaster management should also be taught as a subject in the schools. For working people, we can use websites, flyers, etc. to send them directions how they must prepare for a possible disaster.

2. Special units must be established according to the probabilities of disasters in different areas. For instance, some areas of India are prone to floods. In such areas, boats, a stock of canned foods, medicines, etc. should be kept ready. Similarly, the bomb diffusion units and NSG units must be kept near the terrorism sensitive areas.

3. Mock drills should be conducted to assess how prepared we are to face a disaster. (Such drills have been conducted at the metro stations in Delhi, and they helped the government understand the shortcomings in the plan). In the schools of Japan, children are properly trained how they must evacuate the school building when an earthquake occurs (as earthquakes are too common in Japan).

4. In case of disasters, prevention is better than disaster response, and by acting wisely, we can avoid many disasters. For instance, people must stay vigilant, and when they see any suspicious object, they must tell the police about it because it could be a bomb. Also, the multi-storeyed buildings in the quake sensitive

regions should be made according to the rules applicable on the seismic zones. Fire brigades must be deployed near the major markets and densely populated areas.

5. We should try to develop effective early warning systems (like the ones used in the USA and Japan) so that we can predict the coming disasters like tsunamis, sea-storms, etc. Media can play a vital role in warning the people about a coming or probable disaster.

Our suggestion: Though we can stop some disasters, many will still occur. A well-prepared disaster management system can prove to be a gift. Every Indian needs to pay more attention towards the disaster management programs and should learn the basics of it, because a disaster can occur anywhere and anytime; and when it occurs, it claims human lives and wealth.

90. Tourism in India

India is a very rich state in tourist destinations. On the one hand, nature has gifted India with some of the most beautiful places on earth (backwaters of Kerala, sceneries of Himachal and Kashmir, and forests of Assam being some of them), and, on the other hand, India has also been one of the oldest civilisations on earth, and the relics of the Indian civilisation are scattered everywhere on this land (temples of South India, Tajmahal in Agra and Bodhi Temple in Bihar being some of them). In addition, India is a land of many religions, and the followers of different religions visit their sacred places in India every year.

However, despite this vast treasure, India is far behind many countries in the field of tourism. Many experts believe that India has only utilised a fraction of its huge potential. Tourism, which contributes less than 10% to the GDP of India, can contribute much more.

What should India do to attract tourists:

1. First of all, we should tell the world what we have! People of the world know more about the beaches of Australia and less

about the beaches of South India; people know more about the modern marvel Eiffel Tower and less about world's tallest freestanding brick minaret Qutub-Minar. We need to give people an idea of what they can find in India. We need to educate them the about Indian culture and traditions. The more they know about India, the more they'll come here. We should provide the information about the tourist destinations to the tourists who come here every year, so that these tourists will visit more places in India. In fact, we should open our tourist information centres in the cities of other countries too. We should also organise more events like World trade fairs, Commonwealth Games (and Olympics) in India, as these events tell the world a lot about the host country.

2. We should train the people about how they must behave with the tourists. Those who harm, abuse, mock or bother the tourists, must be punished. We should make better arrangements for the tourists' security in India. When the crimes like murders and rapes happen against the tourists in India, it sends a wrong message to the world.

3. We must keep our tourist spots neat and clean. No tourist would like to visit a dirty place or a beach riddled with trash.

4. Those who scratch the monuments or harm them in any manner, must be punished hard. Those who spit or pee anywhere near a tourist spot, present an ugly picture of our country. Such people must be fined.

5. We must open more guest houses and hotels wherever required, and should also run more buses for the tourists. Tourist infrastructure needs to be improved.

6. Medical tourism is catching up fast in India; the main reason being our thousands of years old medicinal system – Ayurveda. People stay in the resorts that provide the Ayurvedic massage and Panchkarma therapy, and they visit the natural places to de-stress. Many of them also learn Yoga. In this field, there is a lot

of scope. In fact, the tourists from many countries also come to our metros for allopathic treatment, because the medical costs in India are far lower than those in the West. We should try to encourage medical tourism in every possible manner.

Our suggestion: Tourism in India has numerous possibilities. We should not waste the opportunity knocking at the door. We must be proactive in our approach to encourage the tourists to visit our country. Tourism can become a major contributor to our nation's development.

91. Manager and Entrepreneur

Manager and entrepreneur, both play very important role in the world of business. Without either of them, the economy of a nation cannot move ahead. Both are crucial for any business firm. (Steve Jobs was a great entrepreneur and Jack Welch is a great manager-cum-entrepreneur). However, there are differences between their roles, qualities and duties.

Let's talk about those differences:

1. The biggest difference is that a manager takes care of someone else's business, while an entrepreneur takes care of his own business. (Therefore, stakes of an entrepreneur are comparatively high; a big mistake may cost a manager his job and an entrepreneur his business!)

2. An entrepreneur, who has his business located in many cities or countries, may not keep abreast with the latest developments occurring at those places, but the managers taking care of a business are always aware of what's going on around them. Therefore, they help the entrepreneur make an informed decision.

3. An entrepreneur is free to take his own decisions, while a manager has to take decisions according to the guidelines provided to him. For instance, a hotel owner can take the decision to add a

new dish to his menu, but a manager will have to get the owner's approval before taking such a decision.

4. A manager helps an organisation reach its goals and objectives, while an entrepreneur sets goals for himself and his organisation. Entrepreneurship needs a risk-taking attitude.
5. A manager working for a big firm often has all the resources of the organisation available to him, but an entrepreneur needs to either manage certain resources or put own money to buy the necessary resources (at least while starting a firm).
6. Job of a manager is much more secure than the business of an entrepreneur. While every company needs managers, most of the newly started businesses do not survive more than five to ten years.
7. Role of an entrepreneur is a more creative one, while the role of a manager is both creative and supervisory.
8. An entrepreneur is free to make mistakes while a manager is required not to make mistakes.

Companies are now demanding a mix of both!

As the businesses are getting more complex day by day, it has become important for the companies to decentralise the power to take certain decisions (especially in the big firms). Each manager, who is well acquainted with the ground reality of business at his location, is expected to act like an entrepreneur and take the best possible decision for the company. Therefore, the managers are now required to develop the entrepreneurial qualities (innovativeness, risk-taking ability, motivation, leadership, etc.).

92. 'Whole is Greater Than the Sum of Its Parts'

(Note: At first, this topic might not look as important to you, but believe me, this is one of the favourite phrases of many MBA professors and it has good chances to be given as a GD topic; else you can use it as a phrase.)

This was once said by Aristotle (the guru of Alexander the Great) centuries ago, and it carries a deeper meaning. Compare this phrase with '1 and 1 is 11, not two'. The phrase means that when many entities come together to form a bigger entity, the formed entity is more than a collection of smaller entities. For example, an aeroplane can take you places, but if we remove all its individual parts and put them together randomly, can they do the same? No. Even though all the parts are still there, the plane, the bigger entity, is not, because there is no coordination between the parts! Similarly, you are more than just the sum of your body's individual organs!

Compare it to a sports team. When all the players play for their individual goals, the team is likely to lose the match, because the objective of the whole team – winning, is forgotten. A business organisation cannot succeed until all its members do not work for the common goals of the organisation. If everyone in the organisation is working for himself, the business will not go too far.

When people come together for a common goal, they can do wonders. The requirements for this to happen are team work, coordination and team spirit. When the members of a team help each other, the team is bound to succeed, but when they don't, the team is bound to fail sooner or later. That's why, they say 'whole is greater than the sum of its parts'.

It is also known as the concept of 'synergy'.

93. Online Shopping Websites – Their Future in India

Online shopping was considered to be a Western phenomenon until a few years ago; but no more. Eastern countries (India, China, Korea and others) are catching up fast. India has understood the comforts of online shopping, and that's why, the use of online shopping websites is increasing day by day. Not only the grownups, but even the children are ordering their products online (of course, their parents make the payments). Some of the popular online shopping websites in India are EBay India, Home Shop 18, Indiatimes, Rediff,

Flipkart, etc., while the world leader Amazon.com and other global companies also ship products to India. There was a time when people would not buy anything unless they touched a product, felt and assessed its quality, but now the trends are changing.

Why do people use online shopping websites:

1. Earlier, shopping used to be more like a festival. People used to go shopping along with their families. They used to roam the markets, pick the products they wanted to, eat out, and come home with a feeling of happiness. But now the people are so busy that they don't get time for shopping. In many families, both the parents are working and they only get a weekend free, which they may not want to spend on shopping. Online shopping provides a great alternative to direct shopping. All a customer needs to do is visit the website, choose the product he wants, make payments (or select 'Cash On Delivery' option, which enables a customer to pay at the time of delivery of products), and wait for the product to reach his doorsteps. The websites also tell the time by which the product will be delivered.

2. A person doesn't have to waste time and energy in traffic jams or payment lines when he does online shopping. Even the petrol/ diesel expenses come down.

3. Often these websites provide a discount on the MRP of the product. They can do this because they often get the product directly from the manufacturer or the wholesaler, and they don't have to pay for the physical locations (store, showroom, etc.) too. People even buy used, and, thus, low-priced, stuff on the websites. Who would want to lose a chance to save money?

4. On most of the online shopping websites, people can order the products anytime they want to, while the shops have to close after their working hours.

5. Customers get a wider range of products on shopping websites, which may not be possible for any showroom to display or store.

For instance, you may get hundreds of thousands of book titles on a book-selling website, while a bookshop may not store more than a few thousand books at a time. Moreover, a customer can compare a product with many similar products on a website. Some websites even provide ratings given to the products by the users, and make customer reviews available. Thus, customer gets more choice while shopping online.

6. People can get the goods delivered at any location they want to.
7. Now the online sites have started providing the option of exchange or return if the customer is not happy with the product. The deliveryman will himself come and collect the delivered goods. This way they have overcome a great limitation.

Why many people still prefer direct shopping:

1. Many people like to visit the shops and buy the products. They want to touch and feel the quality of a cloth before they buy it. They want to make sure that the shirt they want to buy will look good on them. They like to turn the pages of a book before they buy it. It gives them pleasure and satisfaction.
2. Some people don't like to use credit/debit cards for shopping (especially online) because they're not sure whether this way of shopping is safe. They only use currency notes to buy goods; and many shopping websites do not provide this facility.
3. Some people have traditional relations with a shopkeeper. They simply won't go anywhere else because this person treats them well and gives them the best possible deals (at least, they think so).
4. Many people still don't know about online shopping and its benefits.
5. For many people, shopping is still like a festival they want to celebrate. They want to go out and see the world, feel it, meet people, eat out and come back happy.

Our suggestion: Online shopping websites will have to do a lot of hard work before they can utilise the full potential of the Indian market. A website that doesn't accept cash on delivery or provide a discount, will be in a disadvantageous position. Though it is highly unlikely that online shopping will replace traditional shopping in the forthcoming years, still the websites can do better. Online shopping seems to have a bright future in India.

94. Illiteracy in India

Illiteracy has always been a major problem in India, but, thankfully, the situation is improving (though slowly). In 1947, only 12% Indians were literate (i.e., they could read and write at least one language), while in 2001, 65% people were literate. According to the 2011 census, 74% Indians were literate. Illiteracy is more prevalent among females. (According to the 2011 census, around 65% females and 82% males were literate.) Among our neighbours, we are ahead of Pakistan (literacy rate around 62%) and Nepal, but are far behind Sri Lanka (approx. 90% literacy rate) and China (approx. 95% literacy rate). Among the Indian states, Kerala has the highest literacy rate (approx. 94%) while Bihar has the lowest literacy rate (approx. 64%). Despite the *'Sarva Shiksha Abhiyana'* and other efforts made by the government, we need to go a long way.

Causes of illiteracy:

1. There are many villages that do not have schools (and even if there are school buildings, there are not enough teachers in them). Some schools do not have proper facilities (drinking water, toilets, black-boards, lighting arrangements, etc.) or sufficient number of classrooms. In other words, there are few schools for huge population of students. Due to this, many people don't get a chance to study.

2. The 2011 census data suggests that females are still not encouraged to study. Many parents still believe that the duties of women pertain to home and the girls do not need to study. These mental biases have prevented many girls from going to school.

3. Many poor parents can't afford to pay the school fees of their children. They are more concerned about how to feed them rather than how to make them literate. Moreover, they don't understand the long term benefits of education. To many, education is wastage of time because even if their children study up to the primary level, they won't be able to afford any higher education which can get them a job. To encourage poor people, the government began to provide one-time meals into many government schools.

What should be done about illiteracy:

1. The most important step would be creating awareness among the illiterate people. We should make them understand what they'll get by studying, and how studies will improve their future.

2. Government (and NGOs) should open more number of schools that will provide education at lower costs. Necessary facilities, such as drinking water, light, toilets, etc. must be made available in all the schools. Sufficient number of teachers must be employed.

3. People should understand why education is important for both men and women, poor and rich. Besides providing a job, education also helps a person live a quality life. When people will understand this, they will be encouraged to get educated.

Our suggestion: In literacy, India is behind the global average (84%). It is not good for a nation that boasts of being a major power to have more number of illiterate people than any other nation in the world. Our economy is one of the fastest growing; our literacy rate must also be one of the highest. Only then we will be able to fulfil our dream of making India a developed nation.

95. Poverty in India

Despite all the development that took place in India since our independence, poverty is still a major issue we face. According to some experts, around 22% Indian population lives below the poverty line, while some believe that more than 37% people in India live below the poverty line (some even tell bigger numbers). However, there can be no doubt that millions of Indians earn less than $1.25 a day (World Bank's poverty line figure). Thousands of children die due to hunger and malnutrition every year.

Causes of poverty in India:

1. India has a huge population and this population is continuously increasing. The population is so high that the resources of the country, which are often mismanaged, are not sufficient for so many people. Moreover, many poor people have large families and cannot take good care of them.

2. Unemployment in India is very high. There are never sufficient jobs for the literate and illiterate people. In the absence of an income, the poor people remain poor.

3. The Indian economy depends a lot on the agricultural sector, and the agricultural sector depends a lot on the rains. Whenever there are no (or less) rains, the poor farmers do not get sufficient crops to fulfil their daily needs and pay their debts. Even if the rains are sufficient, the agricultural practices are not efficient enough to take the full advantage of it. The Indian farmers grow fewer crops per hectare when compared with the farmers of the developed nations (Japan, USA, etc.). This is another major cause of poverty.

4. Inflation is another cause of poverty. Sometimes, the inflation rates get so high that poor people either can't afford the daily needs or they need to pay a very large part of their limited income to buy them.

5. Inefficient use of resources is another cause of poverty. India has not been able to harness full potential of its human resources and natural resources. As far as the foodgrains are concerned, millions of tonnes of them get spoiled every year because of mismanagement (they could be made available to the

poor people at the lower rates). Also, there is less investment in the small scale industries and rural industries (like handicrafts, handlooms, etc.).

6. Corruption is another major cause of poverty. It has been estimated that less than 10% of the money allotted for the poor reaches the poor.

7. Liberalisation started late in India; or else economic development would have started much earlier.

How can India eradicate poverty:

1. Firstly, we should take some concrete steps to check the rapid growth of population. Only then our plans to end poverty will become successful. People must understand how it's against their own interests to have more number of children.

2. More number of jobs must be created so that the poor people get more chance to earn money. The *Jawahar Rojgar Yojana* is one of the plans the Indian government had started with a view to reduce poverty in the rural sector.

3. Unemployed people must be educated about self-employment. They can be provided technical training. They must be taught the ways to make money by using the resources available to them.

4. Poor people must be provided free primary education so that they get a chance to make their future bright.

5. Like many developed countries, India should also have a social security program, so that, at least, the basic requirements of a person are fulfilled.

6. Micro-loans can be provided to the poor people so that they can start their own small businesses. This experiment has been successful in Bangladesh where 'Grameen Bank', founded by a famous personality, Mohd. Yunus, provides micro-loans to the poor. It has a very high rate of loan payment too. The

Indian bankers can do the same in India (and some are seriously thinking about the same).

7. Corruption should not be allowed to stop poor people's money reach them.
8. Agriculture should depend less on the rainfall. Linking the rivers and storing the rain water can ensure the supply of irrigation water in turbulent times. Agricultural practices should be improved to increase the production of crops.
9. More investment needs to be made in the small scale industries, rural-based industries, and research in agriculture.

Our suggestion: India needs to go a long way to eradicate poverty completely. Before we succeed in this endeavour, we cannot become a truly developed nation.

96. Is Education System of India Effective?

Education is one of the basic needs for development. How bright a nation's future will be depends a lot on its education system. Therefore, it is extremely important that the education system of a country be effective.

In favour of our current education system:

1. The Indian education system has created the engineers and scientists who work for the most reputed organisations of the world (such as NASA). The Indians are working in almost every major business organisation too (Microsoft being a major employer). The Indian doctors have made a great reputation across the world. This wouldn't have been possible if our education system were no good.
2. India has the world class institutes like IITs, AIIMS and IIMs. The students who pass out of these institutes every year are taken in by the most respected brands and companies of the world. This is another proof that India's education system is effective.

3. The Indian students have proved themselves in various exams conducted all over the world. Many of the GRE, GMAT, IELTS, TOEFL, SAT toppers are Indians. India's competitive exams like CAT, IAS exams, AIPMT, CA exams, Olympiads have been called some of the toughest in the world, and thousands of Indian students pass them every year.

Against our current education system:

1. The Indian education system is quite rigid in the sense that it provides very few career options to the students. After a student has passed the 12th board exams, he can see only three major streams – Science, Humanities and Commerce, while in other countries the students can choose the subjects from two or all the three streams (and even the subjects not covered in these streams). In other words, the students have more subject choices and combinations in other countries. (You can study medicine and History together in the universities of USA). This encourages the students to go abroad and pursue education.

2. India's education system has been designed in such a manner that the courses like Engineering, Medicine and Management have become more popular because they are seen as guarantees of good career, while others (geography, education, history, etc.) are looked down upon, because the students from these streams have quite few career choices.

3. It is alleged that our education system provides more of theory-based education and less of the job-oriented and practical education, and that's why, we have so many unemployed graduates and so few world class businesses in India. Though the top institutes of India create world class managers, engineers and doctors, the other institutes are not considered as good, even in India. It was a news in some newspapers that someone in a major organisation said that only 25% of the Indian engineers were employable in the world class organisations (though it is, no doubt, a disputable statement).

4. It is a fact that the Indian students feel a lot of pressure because of the cut-throat competition to get admission in premier institutes. Recently, the first cut-off reached above 99% in some colleges! How many students would be encouraged by such news? Even in the lower classes, there's a very tough competition and there's a lot of pressure to perform on the students. Many students even commit suicide every year because of this pressure. (Replacing the marks system by grade system could be an answer to this problem.) Many students start taking private tuitions for the IIT entrance exams many years before they take the exam. They get no time for the co-curricular activities and sports. How can we call such a system effective?

5. When we talk about the education system, it is important to talk about the number and condition of the educational institutes. We do not have sufficient institutes, teachers, teaching facilities, etc. to meet the needs of our huge population. That's why, many students go abroad to pursue an education. (This point has been covered in detail in the topic 'Illiteracy in India').

Our suggestion: Though not all is negative about the Indian education system, there's a lot of room for improvement. Our education system should be designed in such a way that it makes more people employable, so that the problem of unemployment comes under control. Also, it must not put too much pressure on the students. Education is a need of everyone, and everyone must be able to get high-quality education in an effective education system.

97. IT Sector of India

It won't be an exaggeration to say that India is a superpower in the field of Information Technology. IT sector contributes more than 7% to India's GDP. India's IT companies, such as Infosys, TCS, HCL have made a reputation in the international market. Millions of Indians work in the IT companies and the companies that provide IT-enabled services (such as BPOs, KPOs, etc.). The IT companies have contributed to the development of the cities like Bangalore, Gurgaon, Noida, Pune, etc. The IT companies earn billions of US dollars for the nation every year. The major competitors of India in IT are China and Philippines.

The reasons behind the success of IT sector in India are – availability of skilled manpower, huge English-speaking population of India, lower human resources costs, the Indians willing to work in shifts, development of Computer education in India, wonderful track record of the Indian IT companies, thousands of talented students passing out from IITs, NITs and the engineering colleges every year, development of telecom sector, etc.

However, after the 2008 global economic crisis, India's IT sector has been facing a lot of challenges. Firstly, the IT sector is hugely dependent on the Western countries for business, and since the West (particularly Europe) is facing an economic slowdown, India's IT sector is also facing problems. The Indian IT companies are getting less business from their Western clients because of the crisis, and their growth is suffering due to this. Moreover, there are talks in the US about giving tax concessions to the companies that create employment in the US instead of creating outsourcing jobs in India (though it may not be a danger because those companies save a lot of money by outsourcing work to India, as the salaries of the employees are much lower here). Even though the economic crisis will subside sooner or later, it will delay the growth of our IT companies. Moreover, fierce competition from other low-cost destinations, such as Philippines and China is growing fast. Some people believe that India has already lost many jobs to Philippines. The Indian bureaucracy also creates hurdles in the path of business with other countries.

Our suggestion: Despite the problems and challenges India's IT industry has been facing presently, the future seems to be bright. As the nation moves forward, IT will be expected to play a bigger role in the health, education, space exploration and other sectors. The economic crisis doesn't stay forever and the situation will improve with time. With talent that India possesses, we need not worry about the future of IT; but certainly some positive steps must be taken to overcome the competition.

98. BPO Jobs as Career

BPO jobs have emerged as a lucrative option for the young people. In India, the BPO companies (both Indian and Western) employ lakhs of people. Many people see a BPO job as a quick money-making activity, while many others see it as a career.

Advantages of a BPO job:

1. Most BPO companies accept graduates (with no prior experience) who can fluidly speak the language in which they need to communicate (mostly English for the international BPOs and local languages for the local BPOs). Some BPOs even accept the 12th pass students.
2. Salaries are pretty good in the BPO jobs. There are few sectors that provide such nice packages to the graduates.
3. By working in the BPO industry, a person can not only overcome his shyness but can also improve his communication skills, which help him for the rest of the life.
4. Training is provided by the BPO companies; so even those, who are not fully confident initially, need not worry.
5. Some BPOs conduct the training of their employees abroad; or they may send their employees abroad for further training or experience. This too makes a BPO job lucrative for the people.
6. The BPO companies often provide cabs and one-time meal to their employees. These are some added advantages.

Disadvantages of a BPO job:

1. Many people may not be able to adjust to the night shifts; for such people, a BPO job may not be the choice.

2. Once you work in BPOs, the career choices for you in the other fields are reduced. Though every company needs good communicators, they may also require the candidate to have a set of specific technical skills. So, it may be a bit difficult to change the fields later on (unless you have been gaining the required skills while working in the BPO sector).

3. It is, no doubt, a bit painful to speak with a foreign accent (at least initially); something you may be required to do in a BPO job.

4. The irate customers may abuse a customer care executive. So, a BPO employee needs to get ready to tackle the angry customers all the time.

5. The society in India isn't well-versed with the BPO jobs. So, many people have a wrong perception about them. Some people think they are the jobs for the less talented people, who can't find other jobs. (It's, no doubt, a myth. Think how much talent you need to sell your product to a customer over phone using the language and accent he knows!)

6. Some people say it's a bit hectic to take so many calls everyday, for months and years. They may find it boring.

Our suggestion: If a person can take the challenges of a BPO job (and also likes the job), he should take one without worrying about what others think about it. With the opportunities growing every year, BPO may be a nice career option for many graduates and undergraduates. Yes, it has the potential to become a career choice for the people.

❑❑❑